T0066040

RELIGION101

FROM **ALLAH** TO **ZEN BUDDHISM,** AN EXPLORATION OF THE **KEY PEOPLE, PRACTICES,** AND **BELIEFS** THAT HAVE SHAPED THE RELIGIONS OF THE WORLD

Peter Archer, MA, MLitt

Adams Media
New York London Toronto Sydney New Delhi

Aadamsmedia

Adams Media
An Imprint of Simon & Schuster, Inc.
57 Littlefield Street
Avon, Massachusetts 02322

For information about special discounts for bulk purchases, please contact Simon & Schuster Special Sales at 1-866-506-1949 or business@simonandschuster.com.

The Simon & Schuster Speakers Bureau can bring authors to your live event. For more information or to book an event contact the Simon & Schuster Speakers Bureau at 1-866-248-3049 or visit our website at www.simonspeakers.com.

Manufactured in the United States of America

7 2023

Library of Congress Cataloging-in-Publication Data has been applied for.

ISBN 978-1-4405-7263-0
ISBN 978-1-4405-7264-X (ebook)

Many of the designations used by manufacturers and sellers to distinguish their products are claimed as trademarks. Where those designations appear in this book and Simon & Schuster, Inc., was aware of a trademark claim, the designations have been printed with initial capital letters.

Contains material adapted from the following titles *The Everything® Classical Mythology Book, 2nd Edition*, by Nancy Conner, copyright © 2010 by Simon & Schuster, Inc., ISBN 978-1-4405-0240-8; *The Everything® Judaism Book*, by Richard D. Bank, copyright © 2002 by Simon & Schuster, Inc., ISBN 978-1-58062-728-3; *The Everything® Kabbalah Book*, by Mark Elber and Max Weiman, copyright © 2006 by Simon & Schuster, Inc., ISBN 978-159337-546-1; *The Everything® Catholicism Book*, by Helen Keeler and Susan Grimbly, copyright © 2003 by Simon & Schuster, Inc., ISBN 978-1-58062-726-9; *The Everything® Christianity Book*, by Michael F. Russell and Amy Wall, copyright © 2004 by Simon & Schuster, Inc., ISBN 978-1-59337-029-9; *The Everything® Understanding Islam Book, 2nd Edition*, by Christine Huda Dodge, copyright © 2009 by Simon & Schuster, Inc., ISBN 978-1-59869-867-1; *The Everything® Koran Book*, by Duaa Anwar, copyright © 2004 by Simon & Schuster, Inc., ISBN 978-1-59337-139-5; *The Everything® Hinduism Book*, by Kenneth Shouler and Susai Anthony, copyright © 2009 by Simon & Schuster, Inc., ISBN 978-1-59869-862-6; *The Everything® Buddhism Book, 2nd Edition*, by Arnie Kozak, copyright © 2011 by Simon & Schuster, Inc., ISBN 978-1-4405-1028-1; and *The Everything® World's Religions Book*, by Robert Pollock, copyright © 2002 by Simon & Schuster, Inc., ISBN 978-1-58062-648-4.

CONTENTS

INTRODUCTION

Religion has, for 5,000 years, been an essential part of the human condition. Spiritual beliefs of all kinds have sought to shape the human psyche and leave a lasting imprint on our souls.

In the pages of this book, you'll stroll through the temples of the Greeks and Romans, marvel at the soaring spires of medieval Christian cathedrals, stand astonished before the graceful minarets of the Blue Mosque in the ancient city of Istanbul, and gaze in wonder at the Borobudur Buddhist temple in Indonesia. You'll read about saints and sinners, heroes and heretics, and the great thinkers, visionaries, and mystics who shaped our spiritual landscape.

Religion is a complicated subject, partly because there are so many shades of religious belief and partly due to the difficulty of actually defining what religion is.

The Concise Oxford Dictionary characterizes it as "the belief in a superhuman controlling power, especially in a personal God or gods entitled to obedience and worship." That's a pretty loose definition and it covers a lot of ground.

Today, there are five major religious traditions: Judaism, Christianity, Islam, Buddhism, and Hinduism. There are countless smaller groups, some of which are subsections of these five and others that have no connection to them. While we can't possibly cover all of them, this book will be a crash course in the main elements of world religion.

Religion has also been a huge source of conflict, from the Crusades of the Middle Ages to the terrorist attacks of September 11, 2001. By understanding one another's belief systems and respecting them, we can avoid such fanaticism ourselves and recognize it when it appears in others.

Religion has created complex philosophies, profound and moving literature, and works of art that dazzle and awe us with their magnificence. These endure, even when the religious beliefs that produced them are no longer actively pursued. Through religion's astounding cultural legacy, we can continue to appreciate it and its contribution to the world.

So get ready for a long, fascinating journey down the path of spiritual enlightenment.

CHAPTER 1
EARLY RELIGIONS

The earliest religious rituals seem to have arisen simultaneously with the development of communities of humans. The cave paintings in Lascaux in France, for example, which were the product of bands of hunters and gatherers, may well have had a religious significance; it's been argued by anthropologists that they are often found in the most remote areas of the caves—where the strongest magic resided. It's possible that creating an image of an animal (particularly an animal that was in the process of being hunted) was an appeal to the Divine to give good fortune to the hunter in his quest for food.

With the rise of settled societies between the Tigris and Euphrates rivers, we find the systematic worship of deities and particular powers ascribed to them. Mesopotamian religion was often dark and gloomy. The hero Gilgamesh in the epic poem of the same name does not look forward to any blessed afterlife; rather, he believes that the afterlife will be full of suffering and sorrow. This may well reflect the tenuous nature of Mesopotamian society.

By the time of the rise of ancient Greece, religious rituals and beliefs were well established, and a special order of people—priests—had been set aside to serve as intermediaries between ordinary people and the gods. The gods of Greece were seen as neither especially benevolent or evil. They just ... *were*. Often they embodied natural phenomena:

GOD	DOMAIN
Zeus	Lightning
Apollo	The Sun
Artemis	The Moon
Poseidon	The Oceans and Seas
Others reflected human concerns and products:	
Aphrodite	Love
Ares	War
Demeter	Grain
Athena	Wisdom
Hestia	The Hearth
Dionysus	Wine and Drunkenness

Unlike later religions (Christianity, Judaism, Islam), the gods were unconcerned with ethical issues. At most, they might punish pride, particularly if it took the form of blaspheming against them. But oftentimes their motivations were unknowable to humans.

> *To mourn avails not: man is born to bear.*
> *Such is, alas! the gods' severe decree:*
> *They, only they are blest, and only free.*
> —Homer, *The Iliad* (trans. Alexander Pope)

People prayed to the gods not for divine guidance but so that either the gods would grant favor to them or—more often—that the gods would leave them alone.

Almost all ancient societies were polytheistic. Even the Jews, who worshiped a single god, Yahweh, did not initially deny the existence of other gods. They were merely exclusive in their worship. Other societies such as the Greeks, the Romans, and the Egyptians worshiped a broad pantheon of gods and seem to have frequently borrowed gods from one another. In the world of the Mediterranean and the East, myths and stories circulated freely, spreading religious beliefs across Europe and Asia.

THE RITES OF DIONYSUS

The God of Disorder

The ancient Greeks were polytheists (that is, they worshiped many gods). These included Zeus, lord of all the gods and bringer of thunder; his wife Hera, goddess of marriage; Aphrodite, goddess of love and beauty; her brother Ares, god of war; and Dionysus, god of wine and revelry.

The religious rites of Dionysus were different from those held to honor other Olympian deities. Traditional rites honored the gods and goddesses in temples specially built for that purpose. Dionysus wandered among the people, and his cults celebrated him in the woods. In Dionysian festivals, worshipers became one with the god. This god loved people; he loved dance; and he loved wine. His festivals were like big parties.

Dionysus was usually accompanied on his travels by the Maenads, wild followers whose name means "madwomen." The Maenads carried a *thyrsus*, a symbol of Dionysus, and incited people to join Dionysus's cult and participate in his rites. Although everyone was invited, women were the most eager participants in Dionysian festivals.

What Was a Thyrsus?

A *thyrsus* was a long pole or rod covered in grapevines or ivy, adorned with grapes or other berries, and topped with a pinecone. It was a symbol of fertility and a sacred object in Dionysian rites.

Dionysus was the god of wine, and his rituals celebrated this drink. It was believed that wine gave people the ability to feel the greatness and power of the gods. Through wine, his worshipers achieved the ecstasy they needed to merge with the god. One of Dionysus's names was Lysios, which meant "the god of letting go." But the excesses of his festivals often led to frenzy and madness.

Dionysian rites were usually held at night. Women dressed in fawn skins, drank wine, wore wreaths of ivy, and participated in wild dances around an image of Dionysus (believed to be the god himself). Sometimes the women would suckle baby animals such as wolves or deer, and sometimes they would hunt down an animal, tear it to pieces, and devour the raw meat. Occasionally, the crazed women would tear apart a man or a child in their rites.

Wine in Ancient Greece

The Greeks have been cultivating grapes for winemaking since the late Neolithic period. As Greek society expanded, so too did its trade in grapes and wines. By the time classical Greek civilization was at its height in the fourth century B.C., the Greeks were exporting and importing wine from as far away as Spain and Portugal.

The wine and tumultuous dancing took worshipers to a state of ecstasy, in which they felt the power of the gods. Religious ecstasy was often heightened by sexual ecstasy. The nights were wild and the followers frenzied—and anything was possible.

Dionysus Takes a Wife

Ariadne, daughter of the Cretan king Minos, was in love with the great hero Theseus. When Theseus came to Crete to kill the Minotaur (a terrifying monster), Ariadne fell in love with him at first sight. Unfortunately, the feeling wasn't mutual.

Ariadne helped Theseus achieve his quest, thus alienating herself from her father. She ran off with Theseus, who promised to marry her when they reached Athens. On their journey, they stopped at the island of Naxos. As Ariadne lay sleeping on the shore, Theseus sailed away and left her.

She awoke alone and friendless on a strange island, abandoned by her lover. But Dionysus saw her and was struck by her beauty. He fell in love with her instantly and made her his wife. Some myths say the couple resided on the island of Lemnos; others say he took his bride to Mount Olympus.

Offspring of the God

Ariadne and Dionysus had many children, including:

- Oenopion
- Phanus
- Staphylus
- Thoas

Oenopion became the king of Chios. Phanus and Staphylus accompanied another Greek hero, Jason, on his quest for the Golden Fleece. Thoas became the king of Lemnos.

Madness Unleashed

Although the Dionysian rites were popular, not everyone accepted them. Some held that Dionysus wasn't truly a god, a claim that stirred his wrath. Just as Hera had punished Dionysus with madness, he punished those who offended him in the same way. Then, he'd watch the afflicted mortal destroy himself.

Dionysus, though a good-time guy, had a short temper and a creative imagination. His punishments were cruel and brutal—and not just for the one being punished. Sometimes, innocent bystanders also got hurt.

The Madness of King Lycurgus

Lycurgus, king of Thrace, banned the cult of Dionysus in his kingdom. When he learned that Dionysus and his Maenads had arrived in Thrace, Lycurgus tried to have Dionysus imprisoned, but the god fled to the sea, where he was sheltered by the nymph Thetis. The king's forces did manage to capture and imprison some of Dionysus's followers.

In retaliation, Dionysus inflicted Lycurgus with madness. With the king unable to rule, the imprisoned followers were released. But that wasn't the end of the story.

The mad Lycurgus mistook his son for a vine of ivy, a plant sacred to Dionysus. In a rage, the king hacked his own son to death. To make matters worse, Dionysus plagued Thrace with a drought and a famine. An oracle revealed that the drought would continue until Lycurgus was put to death. The starving Thracians captured their king and took him to Mount Pangaeus, where they threw him among wild horses, which dismembered and killed him. Dionysus lifted the drought, and the famine ended.

A God Imprisoned

In Thebes, the young king Pentheus banned Dionysian rites. In defiance of the king's decree, Dionysus lured the city's women (including Pentheus's mother and aunts) to Mount Cithaeron, where they took part in a frenzied rite. Pentheus refused to recognize Dionysus's divinity and had Dionysus imprisoned in a dungeon. But the dungeon couldn't hold Dionysus; his chains fell off, and the doors opened wide to release him.

Next, Dionysus convinced the king to spy on the rites held on Mount Cithaeron, promising him spectacular sights and a chance to witness sexual acts. Pentheus hid himself in a tree as Dionysus had instructed. The women taking part in the rites saw Pentheus in the tree and mistook the king for a mountain lion. In a wild frenzy and led by Pentheus's own mother, the women pulled him down and tore him to pieces.

THE ELEUSINIAN MYSTERIES

The Mysterious Heart of Greek Religion

Among the most enduring of Greek myths was that of Demeter and her daughter Persephone.

Hades, god of the Underworld—the realm of the dead—noticed Persephone as she gathered flowers on a plain in Sicily. He was immediately overwhelmed by her beauty, and without bothering to court her he bore her off to his underground realm.

Upon discovering her daughter's abduction, Demeter could not be consoled; she was beside herself with fury, pain, and grief. She abandoned Mount Olympus and her duties as a goddess. Without Demeter's attention, the world was plagued by drought and famine. Plants withered and died, and no new crops would grow.

Demeter's Travels

In her grief, Demeter wandered the countryside. Sometimes she encountered hospitality; other times she met with ridicule. For example, a woman named Misme received Demeter in her home and offered her a drink, as was the custom of hospitality. Thirsty, Demeter consumed her drink quickly, and the son of Misme made fun of her, saying she should drink from a tub, not a cup. Angry with his rudeness, Demeter threw the dregs of her drink on the boy, turning him into a lizard.

Religion 101 Question

The Roman name for Demeter was Ceres. Since she was the goddess of grain, what English word do you think comes from "Ceres"?

In Eleusis, Demeter transformed herself into an old woman and stopped to rest beside a well. A daughter of King Celeus invited her to take refreshment in her father's house. Demeter, pleased with the girl's kindness, agreed and followed her home.

At the king's house, Demeter was met with great hospitality from the king's daughter and the queen. Although Demeter sat in silence and would not taste food or drink for a long time, eventually a servant, Iambe, made her laugh with her jokes.

Demeter became a servant in the house of Celeus along with Iambe. The queen trusted Demeter and asked her to nurse her infant son Demophon. In caring for this baby, Demeter found comfort only a child could give her and decided to give the boy the gift of immortality. To do this, Demeter fed him ambrosia (the sacred food of the gods) during the day and, at night, placed him in the fire to burn away his mortality. But the queen saw the child in the fire and screamed in horror and alarm. Angry at the interruption, Demeter snatched the child from the flames and threw him on the floor.

Demeter changed back into her true form and explained that she would have made the boy immortal, but now he'd be subject to death like other humans. Then, she ordered the royal house to build her a temple and taught them the proper religious rites to perform in her honor. These rites became known as the Eleusinian Mysteries.

Still a Mystery: Eleusinian Rites

The Eleusinian Mysteries were the most sacred ritual celebrations in ancient Greece. The people of Eleusis built a temple in Demeter's honor, where the Eleusinian Mysteries were observed.

The cult was a secret cult, and so it was considered a mystery religion, in which only initiates could participate in rituals and were sworn to secrecy about what happened during those rituals. At Eleusis, stipulations existed about who could be initiated. For example, any person who had ever shed blood could not join the cult. Women and slaves, however, were allowed to participate, even though other sects excluded these groups.

Other Mystery Religions

Besides the Eleusinian Mysteries, ancient mystery religions included the Dionysian cults, the Orphic cults, the Cabiri cults, and the Roman Mithraic cults. These cults were popular and received government support. Starting around the fourth century A.D., however, the spread of Christianity diminished interest in the ancient mystery religions.

The Eleusinian initiates took their pledge of secrecy seriously and were careful to honor it. In fact, they did such a good job of maintaining silence that today's scholars do not know what happened in the Eleusinian rites, although there are many theories. There were two sets of rites: the Lesser Mysteries (which corresponded with the harvest) and the Greater Mysteries (which corresponded with the planting season and took ten days to complete). The Lesser Mysteries were probably held once a year, while the Greater Mysteries may only have been celebrated every five years.

Persephone's Return

After wandering for a long time, Demeter consulted Zeus on the best way to retrieve her daughter. Because of the vast famine caused by her grief, the chief of the gods took pity on her and on the world's people and forced Hades to return the stolen girl. However, the Fates had decreed that if anyone consumed food in the Underworld, he would be condemned to spend eternity there. Persephone had eaten six (some say four) pomegranate seeds and was thus condemned to spend that number of months each year with Hades. During her absence, her mother mourned for her, and the earth was cold and barren. When Persephone returned to the surface, Demeter celebrated, and the earth became warm and fertile with crops.

ISIS AND OSIRIS

God and Goddess Matched in Love and Death

One of the most important and powerful civilizations of the ancient world grew up along the banks of the Nile River in northern Africa. The Egyptians created a society that lasted for 3,000 years, and whose sun-bleached remains may be seen today by visitors to the Pyramids, the Sphinx, and the tombs of the great pharaohs.

The Egyptians worshiped a variety of gods, some of whom they borrowed from other civilizations with whom they came into contact through trade and conquest. A principal feature of their religion was a belief in the divinity of the ruler, the pharaoh. The pharaoh, it was said, was of divine descent and had come down from the sky to rule the people. The Egyptians also believed in the importance of the afterlife, and for this reason, when a pharaoh died his funerary rites were at least as important as any conducted while he was living.

The Egyptians were sun worshipers—not very surprising in a society whose livelihood depended so much on the weather to bring good crops and feed them. Like many ancient people, the Egyptians identified natural forces with particular gods. Among the most important of these gods was Osiris.

Son of Gods

Osiris was said to be the son of the god Geb and the goddess Nut. Geb was the god of the earth, while Nut ruled the sky, so Osiris was the unifying element who made human existence possible. Osiris, it was believed, controlled the flooding of the River Nile, which was the natural phenomenon that made Egyptian civilization vital.

Each year, the Nile floods, depositing a rich silt on the banks, which in turn is farmed by the Egyptians. It's the regularity of this flooding that made it possible for the Egyptians to construct a strong, stable civilization.

Disaster in Mesopotamia

To the east, in the area between the Tigris and Euphrates rivers, another civilization sprang up, that of Mesopotamia. However, while the Tigris and Euphrates also flood, their flooding is irregular and unpredictable, making farming a much more chancy business than in Egypt. For this reason, the gods of Mesopotamia were far more dangerous and feared than those of the Egyptians, reflecting the unstable life of people in this part of the world.

The Greek writer Plutarch tells a version of the mythology of Osiris in which Osiris's brother Set, jealous of him, seized Osiris and shut him in a box, sealed it with lead, and cast it into the Nile. It was rescued by Osiris's wife Isis, who opened the box and brought her husband back to life. The two had a child, Horus, but Osiris later died again, and Isis concealed his body in the desert. There it was found by Set, who tore it into fourteen pieces and scattered them across Egypt. Isis gathered the pieces and buried them. The other gods, impressed by this devotion, resurrected Osiris once again and made him god of the Underworld.

God of the Underworld

As a god of the Afterlife, Osiris presided over a kingdom of those souls who had lived their lives well, in accord with the principles of *Ma'at*, the Egyptian notion of balance and order. All souls, upon death, were judged (a concept later adopted by Christianity) and either delivered to the kingdom of Osiris or subject to punishment for their sins.

The cult of Isis and Osiris lasted for a surprisingly long time—until at least the sixth century A.D. in some parts of Egypt and the Near East. The worship of these deities finally ended when the Roman emperor Justinian (482–565) ordered their temples pulled down and their statues sent to Rome for display.

Religion 101 Question

Osiris's death and resurrection is seen by most anthropologists as clearly related to an annual event that occurred in Egypt. What do you think it was?

The death and rebirth of the land of Egypt each year through the floodwaters of the Nile. The murder and rebirth of the god was reenacted each year by Egyptian priests as a way of placating the gods and ensuring a good harvest.

THE EGYPTIAN CULT OF THE DEAD

The Journey of the Deceased Beyond the Grave

The Egyptians were fascinated by the concept of an afterlife and developed many rituals and practices that were designed to help the soul (*ka*) survive and thrive after death. Many of these spells were contained in the various versions of the *Book of the Dead*, first created about 1700 B.C. and developed in at least four major versions during the next 2,000 years.

According to the *Book of the Dead*, there were a number of different parts of humans including some that survived death.

- The *khat* or physical body, which began to decay with death.
- The *sahu* or spiritual body, into which the *khat* is transformed through prayers of the living.
- The *ka*, usually translated as "soul." This had an independent existence from the body and could move freely from place to place. It could eat food, and it was necessary to provide food and drink for it in the burial chamber. Prayers of the living could also transform food painted on the walls of the burial chamber into food that could be consumed by the *ka*.
- The part of humans that could enjoy an eternal existence was called the *ba*. The *ba* rests in the *ka* and is sustained by it. We might think of it as the spiritual heart of the *ka*.
- The *khaibit* or shadow. Like the *ka*, this could separate itself from the body but was generally in the vicinity of the *ka*.
- The *khu*, or covering of the body. In Egyptian funeral art, the *khu* is often depicted as a mummy.
- The *ren* or name of a man, which existed in the realm of Osiris.

Mummification

One very important reason for mummification in ancient Egypt was to preserve the physical body (*khat*) long enough for it to be transformed into a spiritual body (*sahu*). However, because the process of mummification was prolonged and expensive, most people in Egypt did not undergo it after death.

The Egyptians began to mummify their dead at least as early as 3400 B.C. The process, as it developed over the centuries, went like this:

1. The brain was removed with a hook through the nose, after which the inside of the skull was washed.
2. Internal organs were removed, and the body was stuffed with spices to preserve it.
3. The body was dried for seventy days, using salts to remove moisture.
4. Protective husks were placed over the fingers and toes to prevent breakage; then the body was wrapped first in linen strips, then in canvas.
5. The mummy was placed in a wooden coffin, which was then encased in a stone sarcophagus.

The Pyramids

The pyramids are the most iconic structures associated with ancient Egypt. They are closely bound up with Egyptian veneration of the dead, as well as a demonstration of the awesome power of the ancient pharaohs. The earliest was built between 2630 and 2611 B.C.; the most famous are those at Giza outside Cairo.

Contrary to popular impression, not all pharaohs were interred in pyramids. Tutankhamun, for example, one of the best-known (to us) pharaohs, was buried in an underground tomb in the Valley of the Kings. However, the sheer scale of the pyramids at Giza makes them impressive tributes to the pharaohs who built them.

The largest of these pyramids, the Great Pyramid of Giza, was probably constructed as a tomb for the pharaoh Khufu (c. 2580 B.C.), a ruler of the fourth dynasty.

Impressive Statistics

- The Great Pyramid of Giza was the tallest manmade structure in the world for more than 3,800 years.
- The pyramid consists of 2.3 million limestone blocks.
- The mean opening in the joints between the blocks is 0.5 millimeters.
- 5.5 million tonnes of limestone, 8,000 tonnes of granite, and 500,000 tonnes of mortar were used to build the Great Pyramid.

The Tomb of Tutankhamun

Among the most famous of all Egyptian tombs is that of the pharaoh Tutankhamun (ruled c. 1332–1333 B.C.). The tomb was discovered on November 4, 1922, by the archeologist Howard Carter and, though this was not known until some years later, was entered the night it was discovered by Carter, his patron Lord Carnarvon, and Carnarvon's daughter, Evelyn, who examined it and then left, carefully resealing the door. The tomb had, at some point in the far distant past, been opened by robbers, but the thieves had evidently been caught and the tomb resealed. It was in a remarkable state of preservation; Carter found funeral flowers preserved in the still air (though they dissolved when touched) and could see in the dust on the floor the bare footprints of the workmen who had resealed the tomb.

From the contents of the tomb, archeologists were able to learn much about Egyptian funerary customs. Tutankhamun's body had been placed in a series of coffins, nestled one within the other; one was made of pure gold. The face of the mummy was covered by a golden mask, which became one of the most famous images associated with the pharaoh.

Artifacts preserved from the tomb have toured museums worldwide on several occasions, allowing millions of people to view firsthand this remarkable collection of objects.

THE ROMAN GODS

Borrowing from the Greeks for a Unique Pantheon

Early in Rome's history, the ancient Romans had a religion that was completely their own. As time passed, however, extensive changes occurred within this religion. As Romans conquered neighboring territories, they absorbed some aspects of local religions, and as Greek literature became known in Rome, it influenced Roman religion. Greek mythology was assimilated into Roman mythology to fill in gaps in the latter; eventually, Romans adopted (and adapted) Greek myths on a broad scale.

Although the Romans borrowed heavily from Greek mythology, they kept their own names for the gods and goddesses. To gain a very basic knowledge of Roman mythology, just examine the Roman and Greek counterparts in the following table. Because Roman myths are so similar to Greek ones, knowing the Roman equivalents of Greek names gives you a head start in understanding Roman mythology.

GREEK NAME	ROMAN NAME	GREEK NAME	ROMAN NAME
Aphrodite	Venus	Hephaestus	Vulcan
Apollo	Sol	Hera	Juno
Ares	Mars	Heracles	Hercules
Artemis	Diana	Hermes	Mercury
Athena	Minerva	Hestia	Vesta
Cronus	Saturn	Muses (Musae)	Camenae
Demeter	Ceres	Odysseus	Ulysses
Dionysus	Bacchus	Pan	Faunus
Eos	Aurora	Persephone	Proserpine

Eris	Discordia	Poseidon	Neptune
Eros	Cupid	Rhea	Ops
Fates (Morae)	Parcae	Zeus	Jupiter
Hades	Pluto		

Unlike the Greeks, Roman religion was a highly political affair—not surprising in the world's first great political institution, the Roman Empire. Priests were not separated out from the rest of society and positions within the Roman priesthood were often filled by citizens who had formerly been great soldiers or orators.

Pontifices and Augurs

There were two kinds of Roman priests. The *pontifices* (from which word we get the English word *pontiff*) were the leaders of Roman religious organizations. Their duties included regulation of the Roman calendar and the ceremonies worshiping the various gods. There were fifteen pontifices, and their leader, the Pontifex Maximus, was the head of the Roman religious establishment.

The *augurs*, on the other hand, specialized in divining the will of the gods from elaborate rituals that often (though not always) involved the slaughter of animals. After the sacrifice, having been sprinkled with wine and a sacred cake, was killed, its liver and entrails were examined. From this the augurs could predict the future and, they hoped, gain the favor of the gods. To that end, if any mistake was made in the ritual, the priest had to begin again.

Beginning during the reign of the first emperor, Augustus (63 B.C.– A.D. 14), there grew up a cult of the emperor. After Augustus, all emperors were ritualistically deified and worshiped, and colleges of priests called *augustales* oversaw the worship.

Religion as a Unifier

The Romans administered a vast and diverse empire, one that had begun to grow under the old Republic and reached its zenith under the emperors. In ruling such different peoples with their varied customs, the Romans showed great tolerance of local customs, but they insisted that subjects of the empire recognize the divinity of the emperor. This meant that the cult of the emperor served as a unifying device; it worked particularly well in the eastern regions of the empire, where there was a long tradition of god-kings.

The Divine Origins of Rome

The Romans could not credit the notion that their empire was the result of mere chance. Clearly, the gods must have intended them to emerge as a great power, ruling the Mediterranean world. Various origin stories about Rome grew from legend and myth and were given artistic coherence in the first century B.C. by Virgil, greatest of all Roman poets. Virgil composed *The Aeneid* to both link the beginning of the Roman people to the greatest of all ancient legends—the fall of Troy—and to show that the gods themselves had decreed that Rome would emerge as the greatest city in the world.

> *But next behold the youth of form divine,*
> *Caesar himself, exalted in his line;*
> *Augustus, promis'd oft, and long foretold,*
> *Sent to the realm that Saturn rul'd of old;*
> *Born to restore a better age of gold.*
> —Virgil, *The Aeneid* (trans. John Dryden)

According to Virgil, Prince Aeneas of Troy escaped the destruction of the city at the hands of the Greeks. Bearing his aged father on his shoulders, and leading his little son by the hand, Aeneas made his way from the burning fortress and, with followers, escaped. They spent many years wandering but finally arrived at the mouth of the Tiber River, when they founded a city, Alba Longa. Aeneas married Lavinia, daughter of the local king, Latinus (from which comes the word *Latin*). Their descendants were the founders of Rome.

A Visit to the Underworld

During his wanderings, Aeneas was permitted by the gods to visit the Underworld. There he encountered not just the spirits of the dead but also beheld those waiting to be born. These included the founder of the city of Rome, Romulus; great generals and kings who would lead the city to glory; and the figure of Augustus himself. This last was a not-so-subtle bit of flattery on the part of Virgil, since the poem was written with Augustus's patronage.

THE CULT OF MITHRAS

The Worship of the Bull of Heaven

One consequence of the Roman Empire spreading very far afield was that its soldiers picked up a lot of religious customs from the fringes of Europe and Asia and, eventually, transmitted them throughout the empire. The outstanding example of this kind of religious migration was the cult of Mithras, which reached its height in the fourth century A.D.

Mithras probably started off as a Persian religious figure, though he may also have been worshiped in India under the name Mitra ("the shining one"). He was a sky god, like Zeus and Jupiter, referred to in ancient texts as "the genius of the heavenly light." He was associated with a pantheon of Persian gods that culminated in the supreme deity Ahura Mazda.

The Mithraic Bull

There are many depictions of Mithras in Roman art, but the dominant motif shows him sacrificing a bull. In the telling of this story, the sacrifice is made to the sun god, Sol. The bull has escaped from a burning stable, and while grazing peacefully, it is attacked by Mithras, who seizes it by the horns, mounts and rides it, and eventually casts over his shoulders. In most depictions of the sacrifice, Mithras wears a Phrygian cap (that is, a cap worn by inhabitants of central Turkey). Mithras is often accompanied in his sacrifice by a youth named Cautes.

The story has its origins in a Persian myth that Ahura Mazda created the bull before all else. The bull was slain by the god of evil,

Ahriman, and from the bull's side came the first man, Gayômort, while from its tail came seeds and plants, from its blood the vine, and from its semen all other beasts.

In some depictions of the sacrifice, once Mithras has slain the bull he and the sun god sit down to a banquet. At its conclusion, Mithras mounts a chariot with the sun god and ascends into the sky. Some scholars see similarities to the story of Christ's ascension into heaven.

Spread of the Cult

Like the Eleusinian Mysteries, Mithraism was a mystery religion, so it is difficult to say much about its rituals and practices.

Religion 101 Question

What Christian holiday do some scholars argue was actually an appropriation of the date attributed to the birth of Mithras?

December 25, Christmas Day

What we know for certain is that the cult of Mithras spread with great speed and that it was especially popular with Roman soldiers. The remains of Mithraic temples have been found at the sites of a number of Roman military camps.

ALEXANDER THE GREAT

Creator of Hellenistic Culture

It might seem odd in a book about religion to devote a section to a political and military figure such as Alexander of Macedon. But Alexander's conquest had profound results for all of Greek and Eastern culture, including religion.

Alexander (356–323 B.C.) was the son of Philip of Macedon, king of what had been up to that point a minor realm on the Greek Peninsula. Young Alexander was tutored by the Greek philosopher Aristotle (though it's unclear how much influence this had on him) and succeeded to the throne when his father was assassinated in 336. In the next thirteen years, he would create the largest empire the world to that point had known.

Alexander struck first against the Greeks' old enemy, the Persians. At the battle of Issus in 333, he definitively broke the power of the Persian ruler Darius III and swept over the remnants of the Persian kingdom. He expanded into Egypt, where he founded the city of Alexandria, including its great library (one of the glories of the ancient world).

Alexandria after Alexander

The library of Alexandria became one of the most important repositories of learning in the ancient world. Ships entering the city's port were searched for books; those that were found were confiscated and added to the library's collection (although copies were returned to their owners). The library also contained a zoo and an astronomical observatory. Among the library's holdings were a book by Aristarchus of Samos (310 B.C.–c. 230 B.C.), who first proposed that the earth travels around the sun; and Eratosthenes of Cyrene (c. 276 B.C.–c. 195 B.C.), who correctly calculated the circumference of the globe.

In 326, Alexander invaded India and marched his men as far as the Indus River. He would have gone farther, but his men were close to revolt, and he was forced to turn back. In 323 he died of a fever near the city of Babylon. He was thirty-three years old.

Hellenism

The conquests of Alexander were not merely military; they were cultural as well. Greek culture spread throughout the Mediterranean and beyond. As it did so, it fused with native cultures to form what historians call Hellenism. New gods were added to the Greek pantheon (and Greek gods found their way into the religious practices of Egypt, Persia, and elsewhere).

The impetus for this came from Alexander himself, who was extremely tolerant of and interested in foreign customs. The Greeks identified local gods with their Greek counterparts:

GREECE	EGYPT
Dionysius	Osiris
Demeter	Isis
Apollo	Horus
Zeus	Ammon

The Egyptians deified Alexander and made worship of him part of their daily rituals. (He was also, of course, venerated as the ruler of Egypt.) Contemporary accounts say Alexander sacrificed to Egyptian gods and encouraged the building of new temples.

As he conquered Persia, Alexander followed a similar pattern of tolerating those religious beliefs he found and attempting to integrate them into the Greek religious system. In India he was fascinated by what contact he had with Hindu Brahmins and hermits, although he seems not to have had any interaction with followers of the Buddha, who preceded him by about 200 years.

Overall, Alexander was responsible for one of the greatest expansions of religious belief in world history and for the fusing of complex religious traditions that would continue to influence one another for the next 500 years.

CHAPTER 2
JUDAISM

Judaism is more than just a religion. Jews have been regarded as a "people," a "nation" (though, for most of its existence, one without a homeland), a "race," and a "culture." Consequently, it has never been clear who is a Jew nor what exactly defines "Judaism."

First and foremost, it must be remembered that Judaism is the religion of the Jewish people. Though over the centuries Jews have dispersed among the nations, a strong sense of kinship has remained among them. Some Jews like to think of themselves as "the tribe"; for instance, the Yiddish word *landsman* (countryman) is used fondly to refer to another Jew.

This explains why some Jews feel a connection when introduced to someone who is also Jewish, feel a sense of pride when a Jew is honored for a major accomplishment, or bear an inordinate sense of loss when learning something terrible befell a fellow Jew.

> *To be a Jew means to feel that wherever a Jew*
> *is persecuted for being a Jew—that means you.*
> —Amos Oz, Israeli writer

The "Chosen" People

Judaism teaches that God made an eternal covenant with the descendants of Abraham, Isaac, and Jacob (Israel), and that every Jew participates in this covenant as a part of the Chosen People.

However, being "chosen" by God does not in any way impart a notion of superiority. In fact, according to one rabbinic interpretation, the Hebrews were not the first to be offered God's covenant and to receive the Torah—this took place only after all the other nations turned it down!

Judaism is a living religion that functions in terms of many relationships: between God and the Jewish People; between God and each individual Jew; and among all humans. Judaism is not practiced in a cloistered environment—it is a religion of the community. This is why prayer takes place in groups of ten or more (a *minyan*), and holidays are celebrated in the home, where family and friends gather together.

The Canons of Judaism

There is not a single accepted definition of Judaism acknowledged as absolute dogma. However, Judaism does encompass certain tenets that all religious Jews adhere to. Maimonides, a twelfth-century influential Jewish thinker, outlined these tenets as the Thirteen Principles of Faith.

1. God exists.
2. God is one and unique.
3. God is incorporeal.
4. God is eternal.
5. Prayer is to be directed to God alone and to no other.
6. The words of the prophets are true.

7. Moses' prophecies are true, and Moses was the greatest of the prophets.
8. The written Torah (first five books of the Bible) and the oral Torah (teachings contained in the Talmud and other writings), were given to Moses.
9. There will be no other Torah.
10. God knows the thoughts and deeds of men.
11. God will reward the good and punish the wicked.
12. The Messiah will come.
13. The dead will be resurrected.

It's a Way of Life

It is crucial to remember that Judaism is not merely a set of ideas about the world. Perhaps more importantly, it is a blueprint for a way of life. To follow Judaism means more than praying or contemplating, having faith, or believing in a supreme being or an afterlife. Following the dictates of Judaism means taking action. Jews cannot excuse themselves from this requirement by claiming that one person cannot possibly make a difference in the world. Such an attitude is anathema to Judaism, which emphasizes the significance of the individual.

In the Talmud, the Jews are taught that every person is like a balanced scale—a person's deeds will tip the scale either toward good or toward evil.

A Jew is defined by his actions more than his intentions. It is his actions that bind him to his community and, through it, to the larger human community.
—Elie Wiesel, writer and human rights activist

God holds people responsible for their actions and teaches us to follow His high standards of ethical behavior. His expectations apply to all human beings, even those who have lost contact with God. In Micah 6:8, it is written that God requires that we "do justice ... love goodness and ... walk modestly with ... God."

THE KABBALAH

Source of Jewish Mysticism

The Kabbalah is a mystical tradition within Judaism. Mysticism refers to the belief that personal communication with or experience of God, or the Divine, is possible through intuition or sudden insight rather than through rational thought.

While it is difficult to know the historical origins of Kabbalah with absolute certainty, discovered texts indicate that it surfaced in the late 1100s in southern France in the area of Provence, and soon spread to northern Spain. The first unequivocal kabbalistic text, *Sefer HaBahir*, is written as though it has a readership that is familiar with its kabbalistic terminology, even though such terms had never appeared in writing before. The earliest Kabbalists speak of the oral transmission of secret knowledge from master to disciple throughout the generations, so there was evidently a kabbalistic community already in existence when *Sefer HaBahir* was written.

What's It Mean?

The term *Kabbalah* comes from the Hebrew root word *l'kabel,* which means "to receive," so *Kabbalah* means "received teachings." *Kabbalah* also denotes "tradition," meaning a body of knowledge and customs passed down from one generation to another. Kabbalah also has the connotation of the *oral* transmission of tradition and knowledge containing the inner and secret mystical teachings of the Torah.

Despite the fact that Hebrew had ceased to be the spoken language of the Jews even before the destruction of the Second Temple in Jerusalem by the Romans in A.D. 70, the vast majority of kabbalistic texts are written in Hebrew. A particularly striking exception for the history of Jewish mysticism is that the most influential kabbalistic text of all, the *Zohar*, is mostly written in Aramaic. Since the *Zohar* is so heavily quoted in later sources, it is very common to find Hebrew kabbalistic texts from the end of the 1200s sprinkled with Aramaic phrases. Over the centuries some kabbalistic texts were translated into other languages such as Latin beginning in the late fifteenth century. In our own day some kabbalistic texts are finding their way into English translations of varying quality.

In the thirteenth century, Spanish Kabbalists spoke of the Torah existing on four different levels. Moshe de Leon coined the term *Pardes* to refer to these four levels.

Pardes, which literally means "orchard" but also has the connotation of Paradise, refers to mystical knowledge.

Moshe de Leon treated this term as an acronym for the four levels of reading Torah. Each of the consonants in the word Pardes stands for one of the levels of meaning in the Torah. The *p* stands for *pshat* or the simple, literal meaning of the words. The *r* stands for *remez*, which means "hint," but in medieval Hebrew came to stand for the allegorical reading of the text that was the mainstay of Jewish philosophy. The *d* stands for *d'rash*, which essentially means "to investigate, to seek out, to expound" and here refers to Aggadic and Talmudic interpretations. The *s* stands for *sod*, the secret meaning of the text. Kabbalah itself is understood as constituting this secret meaning of the Torah.

All the levels of the Torah complement each other. Kabbalists often use the analogy of a nut to visually communicate the relationship between these levels. The outer shell conceals the soft, deep core that is the most nourishing part of the nut.

An Unsolved Mystery

Some of the most basic questions about *Sefer HaBahir* remain unanswered. The *Bahir* is acknowledged by all modern scholars as the first true work of Kabbalah because it contains the major elements that distinguish Kabbalah from other, earlier forms of Jewish mysticism. While traces of the earlier mystical traditions are evident in the *Bahir*, a new literature had clearly emerged. Although it is unclear where the book first appeared, it may have been in Germany in the area where another very important mystical school flourished. This other school was called Hasidei Ashkenaz, which means the German Pietists (that is, very pious people), and is also known as the Hasidim of Medieval Germany. The other possible location of the *Bahir*'s origin is Provence in southern France. The latest research points toward a German origin with a later editing stage in Provence.

It is a common assertion among Kabbalists that God and Torah are one. In other words, Torah at its deepest level contains the essence of divinity. What exactly does this mean?

By equating the Torah with God's essence, Kabbalists emphasize the primacy and strength of language in Judaism. The power of language is evident in the Creation story in Genesis, where it says, "Let there be ... and there was."

The perception that God and Torah are one lends a completely new meaning to the study of Torah. Recognizing the spiritual power of the letters of the Torah makes meditating on a passage of Torah particularly potent. For Kabbalists, texts are important and are to be meditated upon. Studying a spiritual text is not like reading a novel or a history book. There is a layering of words, a trait of kabbalistic literature that becomes more apparent the more times you go over the same passages. Re-examining a certain passage and using it as a focus of meditation can suddenly reveal its many meanings to you. All of this is part of altering your consciousness, the result of spiritual meditation.

Heavenly Messengers: Maggidim

One more avenue of attaining secrets of Torah is through the phenomenon of maggidim. The term *maggid* has numerous meanings, the most common of which is the "traveling preacher." However, in this case a maggid is a disembodied heavenly messenger that visits someone to reveal secrets of Torah and often appears as a voice emerging from the person visited by the maggid. Probably the most famous maggid is the one that appeared with regularity to Rabbi Yosef Karo. Historically, this phenomenon began to be spoken of during the sixteenth century. A number of well-known Kabbalists were visited by maggidim. In addition to Yosef Karo, Rabbi Moshe Chaim Luzzatto and the Vilna Gaon also claimed to have been visited by maggidim.

Understanding with Your Heart

An important thing to understand when speaking about things such as the Torah being all names of God and other striking statements is that these are not intended as intellectual concepts. This is part of the esoteric nature of Kabbalah. When these statements remain "ideas" or "concepts," they are truly hidden. It's only when one begins to experience what is implied by these words that Kabbalah ceases to be a cerebral activity and becomes a much more spiritual one. The process is achieved, if ever, by entering the lifestyle of contemplative study, meditation, kavana (awareness), and so on. As Pirkei Avot (one of the tractates of the Mishna) says, "it's not study that is most important, but practice" (1:17).

Ein Sof and the Sefirot

Kabbalah embodies two major experiences of Divinity. One is that God is transcendent, eternal, and unchangeable. The other is that God is also deeply personal, in other words, the very same Transcendent One is also dynamic and immanent throughout Creation. Kabbalah depicts these two perspectives through the terms *Ein Sof* and the *Sefirot*.

Rabbi Meir Ibn Gabbai explains that we cannot grasp Ein Sof—a term first used by Isaac the Blind, which literally means "without end," or "infinite"—through contemplation or logic. The ultimate nature of God is beyond our grasp, though we may experience a glimpse of that reality and recognize the existence of that which is so far beyond our comprehension. Ein Sof itself is a negative formulation, meaning that there is no end. This is similar to Maimonides's explanation that we can only say what God is not, because God transcends our human ability to define. To define is to limit, whereas God is limitless. The Kabbalists understood that Ein Sof is beyond language and thought, so nothing could actually be said about it.

The Cosmic Influence of Our Acts

Part of what may account for Kabbalah's impact on Judaism and its prominent position for a number of centuries is that it invigorated the everyday acts of people by attributing cosmic influence to them. Kabbalists understand their *kavana*, meaning a person's focus and consciousness, as having an effect beyond their immediate obvious influence. Though people have always had to grapple with the clear lack of connection between a person's moral qualities and their fate and fortune in this world, Kabbalah teaches that our actions have an impact, nevertheless, in ways that are not plainly evident.

Religion 101 Question

Who are some famous Americans who adhere to Kabbalah?

Madonna, Demi Moore, and Ashton Kutcher are among the celebrities who say they have been influenced by Kabbalah.

BRANCHES OF JUDAISM

Orthodox, Reform, Conservative

Throughout history, various movements in Judaism have sometimes split up, like different branches growing from a trunk of the same tree. The oldest records we have of an explicit difference of opinion took place in the second century B.C. In that period Jews lived under Greek occupation. The Greeks were an enlightened people and tolerant of their subjects. As a result, many Jews were attracted to Greek culture, known as Hellenism. Those Jews who allowed themselves to be influenced by Hellenism were known as Hellenistic Jews; the Hasideans (not to be confused with Hasids) formed their conservative opposition.

Essenes, Sadducees, and Pharisees

At a later period in history, when Rome conquered the lands of the ancient Israel, Judaism had split into three sects:

- The Essenes formed an ascetic and mystical order that consisted mostly of adult males who took an oath of celibacy.
- The Sadducees embraced some of the Hellenistic elements of Judaism.
- Pharisees, the most powerful group among the Jews, believed that both the written and oral Torah came directly from God and were therefore valid and binding. In accordance with the Torah, the Pharisees began to codify the Halakhah (the Law), insisting upon its strict observance.

Origin of the Synagogue

Because of their disagreements with the Sadducees, who had control of the Temple, the Pharisees developed the synagogue as an alternative place for study and worship. Their liturgy consisted of biblical and prophetic readings and the repetition of the *Shema* (Judaism's central prayer).

The Orthodox

What ultimately did lead to divisions within Judaism was the same old controversy, that is, the difference of perceptions concerning the Halakhah and the Torah. During the last millennium and up until the nineteenth century, the Orthodox branch of Judaism was by far the most prevalent.

The essential principle governing Orthodox Judaism is *Torah min Hashamayim*. This means that the Torah, both the written Law (Scriptures) and the oral Law (rabbinic interpretation and commentaries), is directly derived from God and therefore must be obeyed.

Synagogue services are conducted in Hebrew and men and women sit separately. Women are not ordained as rabbis, nor do they count in a *minyan* (the group of ten necessary for public prayer). While the synagogue is the domain of men, women clearly have dominion over the home.

When Jews were segregated in ghettos or the "pale of settlement" (regions in Russia that were designated for Jews to inhabit), they had no access to the secular society of the "outside world." They therefore led their lives according to the customs that had been practiced for generations before them.

As the Enlightenment spread through Europe in the seventeenth and eighteenth centuries, many societies began to open at least some of their doors to Jews. Suddenly, Jews now had access to new ideas and new occupations; the barriers that had encased their own closed society were broken down.

Strict observance of Halakhah made it difficult, if not impossible, to integrate into secular society. Moreover, many Jews incorporated aspects of the Enlightenment into their own way of thinking. Such were the circumstances that brought forth Reform Judaism.

Reform Judaism

In the early nineteenth century, several synagogue congregations in Germany instituted fundamental changes in the service, including mixed-gender seating, a shortened service, use of the vernacular in the liturgy, single-day observance of holidays, and the inclusion of musical instruments and a choir.

American Reform Judaism was born when some of these reformers immigrated to the United States from Germany in the mid-nineteenth century. Under the leadership of Rabbi Isaac Mayer Wise, Reform Judaism became the dominant belief held by American Jews.

Reform Judaism in America

Some of the first Reform congregations in the United States:
- Beth Elohim in Charleston, South Carolina (1825)
- Har Sinai in Baltimore, Maryland (1842)
- Bene Yeshurun (I.M. Wise) in Cincinnati, Ohio (1854)
- Adath Israel (The Temple) in Louisville, Kentucky (1842–43)
- Keneseth Israel in Philadelphia, Pennsylvania (1856)

Principles of Reform Judaism

Along with the great deal of room it offers for individualism, Reform Judaism includes the following beliefs:

1. The Torah was divinely inspired but authored by humans.
2. There is only one God.
3. The reinterpretation of Torah is continuous and must be adapted for new circumstances and challenges.
4. The moral and ethical components in the Torah are important.
5. The sexes are to be treated equally.

Conservative Judaism

Despite its many supporters, some Jews felt that Reform Judaism had admirable intentions but that it simply went too far. Out of this middle-ground movement came Conservative Judaism.

Like Reform Jews, Conservatives believe that written and oral Torah were divinely inspired but authored by humans—that it does not come to us directly from God. Conservative Judaism parts with Reform in that it generally accepts the binding nature of Halakhah. However, Conservatives agree that Halakhah is subject to change and that adaptations may be made to it based on the contemporary culture, so long as the Halakhah remains true to Judaism's values.

In the synagogue service Conservative Judaism has provided a distinct middle ground for Jews who are not satisfied with either the Orthodox or the Reform approach. Hebrew is the predominant language of the liturgy, but the native language of the worshipers is used as well. In Conservative congregations, men and women may sit together, and many Conservative congregations have choirs and even organs.

Reconstructionism

This is Judaism's youngest movement. It germinated from an eloquent and momentous article written by Mordecai Kaplan (1881–1983) in 1920, in which he called for a reinterpretation of Judaism in keeping with modern thought and the strengthening of ties with Jewish communities in Palestine. Two years later, he resigned from the pulpit of a Conservative congregation in Manhattan and founded a congregation based on his philosophy of Judaism that came to be known as the Society for the Advancement of Judaism (SAJ).

Kaplan had no desire to create a new branch of Judaism, but given his unique philosophy, this was inevitable. As of the 1970s, Reconstructionism has been recognized as the fourth branch on the Judaic tree. It remains the smallest movement, with 100 congregations worldwide, but its impact belies its numbers, given Kaplan's legacy and the philosophy developed by his followers.

Reconstructionists reject the notion that the Jews are God's "chosen people." Each culture and civilization, Kaplan postulated, has a unique contribution to make to the greater human community. Judaism is only one of these cultures. There is nothing special or divine about it.

Furthermore, Halakhah need only be observed if one chooses to do so; if a person does follow an aspect of Halakhah, this is not because it is binding law from God but because it is a valuable cultural remnant. In fact, the entire notion of a supernatural God acting in history is discarded. Instead, God is considered to be a process or power—an expression of the highest values and ideas of a civilization.

Kaplan taught that Judaism is more than a religion. It's an evolving religious civilization that incorporates traditions, laws, customs, language, literature, music, and art. While he believed in the need for all Jewish communities to thrive in the Diaspora, Kaplan foresaw a Jewish state as the hub on the Jewish wheel. Therefore, Zionism and the establishment of Israel have always been fundamental to Reconstructionism.

HEBREW AND YIDDISH

The Languages of the Chosen People

Hebrew is one of the world's oldest languages, dating perhaps as far back as 4,000 B.C. The early Israelites conversed in Hebrew, a Semitic idiom of the Canaanite group that includes Arabic. The patriarchs spoke Hebrew as they made their way into the Promised Land, and it remained the language of the Israelites throughout the biblical period.

However, in the fifth century B.C., when Jews began to return to Israel from Babylon, where many had lived after the destruction of the First Temple in 586 B.C., most of the inhabitants of Palestine conversed in Aramaic, which gradually infiltrated the language of the Israelites. A few centuries later, Hebrew had all but ceased to exist as a spoken language. It would not be re-established as such for two millennia.

Learn Hebrew

If you would like to learn Hebrew, there are books and websites available to you and courses that you can take. As a matter of fact, there are intensive courses in conversational Hebrew of which you may avail yourself, should you be planning a visit or a stay in Israel and desire to be fluent in its vernacular language.

Writing in Hebrew

Hebrew is read from right to left, just the opposite of reading English. You have to learn a new alphabet, which consists of twenty-two consonants, five of which assume a different form when they appear at the end of a word. And if this isn't enough of a challenge, Hebrew is generally written without vowel sounds!

ד פ ל ח ה ב ק ו
נ ז א ב כ י ג
ו ו ש מ פ ש ט צ
ס ר כ ת

In contrast to the block print that is customarily seen in Hebrew books, sacred documents are written in a style that uses "crowns" on many of the letters. These crowns resemble crows' feet that emanate from the upper points. This type of writing is known as "STA'M" (an acronym for *Sifrei Torah*, *Tefillin*, and *Mezuzot*).

A more modern cursive form of writing is frequently employed for handwriting. Yet another style, Rashi script, appears in certain texts to differentiate the body of the text from the commentary. This kind of text, named in honor of Rashi, the great commentator on the Torah and Talmud, is used for the exposition.

Why More Than One Spelling?

Hebrew words are spelled out in English letters according to a transliteration system, and there is more than one system to choose from. For example, the distinctive throaty Hebrew *h* is sometimes transliterated as *ch*, so the word *Hanukah* may be spelled as *Chanukah*, as it is in this book.

Hebrew Letters Have Numerical Values

The Hebrew numerical system uses letters as digits. Each letter of the alphabet has a corresponding numerical value. The first ten letters have values of one through ten; the next nine have values of twenty through 100, counting by tens; and the remaining letters have values of 200, 300, and 400, respectively.

Since every Hebrew word can be calculated to represent a number, Jewish mysticism has been painstakingly engaged in discerning the hidden meanings in the numerical value of words. For example, the numerical value of the Hebrew word *chai* (life) is eighteen. Hence, it is a common practice to make charitable contributions and give gifts, especially for weddings and bar/bat mitzvahs, in multiples of eighteen.

Modern Hebrew

In the nineteenth century, Hebrew underwent a renaissance. Thanks in large part to Eliezer ben Yehudah (1858–1922), who dedicated himself to the revival of Hebrew and introduced thousands of modern terms to the ancient language, Hebrew regained its status as a vernacular language.

The Roots of Yiddish

Yiddish can trace its roots to the beginning of the second millennium, when Jewish emigrants from northern France began to settle along the Rhine. These emigrants, who conversed in a combination of Hebrew and Old French, also began to assimilate

German dialects. The written language consisted completely of Hebrew characters.

At the beginning of the twelfth century, after the horrific pogroms of the First Crusade, Jews migrated to Austria, Bohemia, and northern Italy, taking their new language, Yiddish, with them. When Jews were invited to enter Poland as traders, Yiddish incorporated Polish, Czech, and Russian language traits. As an end result, Yiddish was composed mostly of Middle/High German, with a measure of Hebrew and touches of Slavic tongues and Loez (a combination of Old French and Old Italian).

Yiddish and Jewish

Jews do not speak "Jewish." Just because *Yiddish* means "Jewish" in the language of Yiddish, these words are not synonymous. *Jewish* is an adjective, while *Yiddish* is a noun that describes a particular Jewish language.

Yiddish served the Jewish people well because it was an adaptable and assimilative language. Consequently, even English words and phrases made their way into Yiddish after the waves of immigration into the United States by European Jewry in the late nineteenth and early twentieth centuries.

Who Spoke Yiddish?

The Yiddish language was the chief vernacular of Ashkenazic Jews (that is, Jews from Central and Eastern Europe), but not all Ashkenazic Jews spoke Yiddish. The language for prayer and study remained Hebrew, although Yiddish was often used in *yeshivas* (religious schools) to discuss the texts. The fact that Yiddish had to do with the daily task of living is reflected in the language itself, and this is one of the factors that makes Yiddish such a unique and alluring language.

The Mother Tongue

Since Jewish women were not taught Hebrew, they spoke Yiddish to their children, who, in turn, later spoke it to their own children. Thus, Yiddish became known as *mame loshen*, the "mother's language," as opposed to Hebrew, *loshen ha-kodesh*, or "the sacred language."

Yiddish is a very social language, replete with nicknames, terms of endearment, and more than a good share of expletives. You will find proverbs and proverbial expressions, curses for just about every occasion, and idioms reflecting the fears and superstitions of the times. To learn and know Yiddish is to understand the Jews who created and spoke the language hundreds of years ago.

The most important factor in the rapid decline of Yiddish in the twentieth century was the *Shoah* (Nazi Holocaust), which destroyed entire communities of Yiddish-speaking Jews. In Israel Yiddish was frowned upon as a language of the "ghetto" that reflected a subservient mentality.

However, in recent decades Yiddish has shown itself to be as stubborn and resilient as the Jewish people themselves. In the United States, colleges and universities offer Yiddish courses, and special organizations and groups promote Yiddish both in the United States and in Israel.

THE TORAH, THE TALMUD, AND THE MIDRASH

The Writings of Judaism

Religious study has always been greatly revered in the Jewish tradition, and there is much to study, such as the Torah, Talmud, the Midrash, and other important texts.

The Torah

The word *Torah* is sometimes translated as "the Law." It also means "a teaching," because it represents God's instructions regarding how Jews should live and what they ought to believe.

In its most limited sense, the Torah comprises the Five Books of Moses, also called the Pentateuch. However, in its broadest sense, Torah encompasses everything that follows the Pentateuch—the whole body of Jewish law and teachings.

In its most general sense, the Torah is composed of two parts. First, there is the written Torah (*Torah Shebichtav*), which in turn has three parts. The first part is the Pentateuch, also known as the Five Books of Moses or *Chumash*. The Pentateuch includes the following five books (named for the first phrase in each book):

1. *B'reishit* (Genesis)
2. *Shemot* (Exodus)
3. *Vayikra* (Leviticus)
4. *Bamidbar* (Numbers)
5. *Devarim* (Deuteronomy)

The second part of the written Torah is *Nevi'im* (Prophets), which contains the following eight books:

1. *Yehoshua* (Joshua)
2. *Shoftim* (Judges)
3. *Shmuel* (Samuel I and II)
4. *Melachim* (Kings I and II)
5. *Yirmiyahu* (Jeremiah)
6. *Yechezkel* (Ezekiel)
7. *Yeshayahu* (Isaiah)
8. *Trey Asar* (the Twelve)

Finally, the third part of the written Torah is the *Ketuvim* (Writings), which consists of eleven books:

1. *Tehillim* (Psalms)
2. *Mishlei* (Proverbs)
3. *Iyov* (Job)
4. *Shir Ha-Shirim* (Song of Songs)
5. *Ruth*
6. *Eichah* (Lamentations)
7. *Kohelet* (Ecclesiastes)
8. *Esther*
9. *Daniel*
10. *Ezra and Nechemiah*
11. *Divrei Ha-Yamim* (Chronicles)

The Oral Torah

In addition to giving Moses the written Torah, God also provided explanations that are called the *Torah Sheb'al Peh* or the oral Torah. These exegeses, which were not written down, were meant to be passed from teacher to student.

From God to the Torah

God transmitted the Torah to His chosen people through Moses. Beginning around the year A.D. 200, the oral Torah was inscribed into a series of books called the Mishna.

It is axiomatic in Judaism that the Torah is everlasting and immutable. Since Torah comes from God and God is eternal, it follows that the Torah also shares this feature.

This is one reason Judaism takes upon itself the responsibility to be true to the Torah and to maintain it as part of the Jews' very existence. According to Judaism, God chose the Hebrews for the task of receiving and preserving the Torah, and this task cannot be abrogated.

The Talmud

In the years after the destruction of the Second Temple (A.D. 70), there was a danger that the oral Law, passed down from teacher to student, would be forgotten. In order to prevent this from happening, a group of scholars and jurists, led by Rabbi Yehuda Ha-Nasi (died c. 217), assembled a basic outline of the oral Law into the Mishna by about 200.

A Saintly Rabbi

Rabbi Yehuda Ha-Nasi was variously addressed as Rabbi, Rabbi Judah the Prince, and our Master the Saint. He was referred to as "Rabbi" because he taught the Torah; he was designated "the Prince" because he was elevated and made the prince and most honored of Israel; he was called "our Master the Saint" because it was said that his body was as pure as his soul.

But the students and scholars of Torah had not completed their work. Over the next several hundred years, they continued to seek explanations for the text and its laws. Once again, in order to keep the results of their efforts from being lost, Rav Ashi (352–427) and Ravina (died 421) guided the compilation of the material into the Gemara. Together, the Mishna and Gemara form what we know as the Talmud.

The Talmud is a record of the way rabbis and scholars and jurists have applied the laws of the Bible to the life they faced. Consequently, it covers "all of life" because it encompasses everything that went on in those people's daily existence. Themes include the social and the private, urban and rural, civil and criminal, public and domestic, everyday and ritual. Virtually nothing was overlooked.

Two Talmuds

There are actually two Talmuds—the Jerusalem Talmud and the Babylonian Talmud. Generally, when people speak of the Talmud, they are referring to the more comprehensive of the two, the Babylonian Talmud.

Organization of the Talmud

The Talmud is divided into six sections called *sedarim* (orders). Each *seder* contains several books called *masekhtot* (tractates); in total, there are sixty-three *masekhtot*. Although the respective *sedarim* seem to address rather specific and narrow topics, each *seder* in fact contains diverse and assorted subjects.

The six *sedarim* are the following:

1. *Zera'im* (seeds): This *seder* deals primarily with agricultural laws but also laws of prayer and blessings; it is comprised of eleven *masekhtot*.
2. *Mo'ed* (season): This *seder* addresses *Shabbat* and festivals; it includes twelve *masekhtot*.
3. *Nashim* (women): This *seder* deals with the laws of marriage and divorce; it contains seven *masekhtot*.
4. *Nezikin* (damages): This *seder* deals with civil law and ethics; it contains ten *masekhtot*.
5. *Kodashim* (holy things): Sacrifices and the Temple are considered in this *seder*, which includes eleven *masekhtot*.
6. *Toharot* (purities): This *seder* deals with laws of ritual purity and impurity, and contains twelve *masekhtot*.

A Work of Many Genres

Despite the fact that it deals with legalisms and extremely specific issues, the Talmud is not a code or catechism that lays down the law in summary, categorical form. In fact, the Talmud is filled with legend, folklore, parables, reminiscences, prayers, theology, and theosophy.

The Talmud is the end result of a process by means of which the law is made clear. Hence, the tensions, conflicts, and arguments of its collaborators come alive before the reader's eyes.

The Midrash

Between the third and twelfth centuries, rabbis and religious scholars compiled ideas and arguments in the form of stories that sought to explicate and probe even deeper the underlying truths and meanings of the biblical text. These stories eventually became known as the Midrash.

In the Midrash, each interpretive story is designed to expand on incidents in the Bible, to derive principles and laws, or to offer moral lessons. Moreover, because of their nature, *midrashim* can be used to gain a glimpse into the way the rabbis read the biblical text and into their thinking processes.

What's It Mean?

The Hebrew word *midrash* translates as "commentary" or "interpretation." It is based on a Hebrew root meaning, "to investigate" or "to study." *Midrash* is a method used to inquire into what a biblical text might mean.

Some Midrashim

Many *midrashim* deal with the story of Creation. For example, when God was ready to create man, He said, "Let us make man." But who is "us"? Wasn't God alone? The *midrash* explains this by concluding that, indeed, God was not alone and that God consulted with the ministering angels.

In contemporary times, there is much controversy over the matter of capital punishment. But the issue is raised much earlier, in the biblical story of Cain killing his brother Abel. While the Bible does allow for capital punishment, God does not inflict this penalty upon Cain. Why not?

The *midrash* addressing this question suggests that since Cain had never witnessed death, he could not possibly have known how his physical assault on Abel would culminate. Therefore, it would not be just to have taken Cain's life—that's why he was sentenced to permanent exile instead. In modern legal jargon, this equates to American and English jurisprudence, where there is a distinction between involuntary manslaughter and voluntary manslaughter as well as among other degrees of murder.

JEWISH HOLY DAYS

Celebrations of Triumph and Tragedy

The Jewish Holy Days begin with the Days of Awe, a ten-day period that generally falls sometime in September or October. These include Rosh Hashanah and Yom Kippur. Other important holidays include Chanukah, Purim, and Passover.

Rosh Hashanah

The phrase "Rosh Hashanah" emerged sometime during the Talmudic times (the first five centuries A.D.). However, the holiday itself was well established by the fourth century B.C., when some Jews had returned from exile to Jerusalem to construct the Second Temple.

Given the importance of this period, preparations for the Days of Awe begin in the preceding month of *Elul*, when it is customary to blow the *shofar* during weekly services in synagogue.

What's a Shofar?

A *shofar* is a trumpet made of a ram's horn. In biblical times, blowing the shofar heralded important events such as holidays, the new moon, or preparation for war. It is also symbolic of Abraham's aborted sacrifice of Isaac, when a ram was offered in Isaac's stead.

As the month of *Elul* draws to an end, there is a special *Selichot* (forgiveness) service on the Saturday night before Rosh Hashanah, when the congregation recites a series of important prayers. Around midnight, the congregation reviews the thirteen attributes of God, a ceremony that helps to prepare everyone for the approaching holy days.

Yom Kippur

Yom Kippur, the last of the Days of Awe, is observed on the tenth of *Tishri*. While *Shabbat* is the holiest of days, it is only human nature to regard Yom Kippur, which occurs only once a year as opposed to once a week, as something very special and out of the ordinary.

Yom Kippur is the "Day of Atonement." It is a day to atone for the sins of the prior year. Yom Kippur is sometimes referred to as the "Sabbath of Sabbaths" and has been an integral part of Judaism for thousands of years.

Fasting is an important part of Yom Kippur. Refraining from consuming food or liquid is a concrete expression of the gravity of the day. It helps each person attain the state of mind required to focus on the spiritual. Furthermore, fasting manifests a form of self-mastery over bodily needs. Another more socially conscious justification states that by fasting, people can identify more readily with the poor and the hungry.

No Young Children, Please

Jews need to observe the mitzvah to fast as long as it does not pose a physical threat. Children under the age of nine and women in childbirth (that is, from the time the labor commences to three days following the birth) are absolutely not permitted to fast. Older children, not yet bar or bat mitzvah, and women from the third to the seventh day after childbirth, are permitted to fast, but should resume eating or drinking if they feel the need.

Chanukah

In 167 B.C., the Greek king Antiochus IV attempted to force the Jews to officially adopt Greek practices. His edicts included the banning of all practice of Judaism, the placement of a Hellenist (a Sadducee) in control of the Temple, desecration of the Temple by requiring the sacrifice of pigs on the altar, and killing those who refused to obey. The time was ripe for rebellion.

The Maccabean Rebellion

Mattityahu (Mattathias) was an elder and religious leader of the distinguished Hasmonean family who lived in Modiin. Resisting the efforts of the Greek army to establish a pagan altar, he launched an uprising against them. Mattityahu and his five sons became known as the Maccabees, which in Hebrew means "men who are as strong as hammers." Though much smaller than the mighty Greek armies, the Jewish forces under the command of Judah Maccabee ultimately triumphed. On the twenty-fifth day of Kislev (the first day of Chanukah), the Maccabees reclaimed the Temple. It was a victory of the oppressed over the oppressors.

When the Jewish forces recaptured the Temple Mount, they wanted to rededicate the Temple. (In fact, *Chanukah* is the Hebrew word for "dedication.") Part of the rededication ceremony required lighting the Temple Menorah, but the Jews could find nothing more than a small quantity of suitable oil, enough to last for one day.

The day after the battle for the Temple Mount, a rider was dispatched to Mount Ephraim, where olive trees grew that provided the oil for the Menorah. It would take three days to reach his destination and three days to return, plus the day needed to press the oil. Meanwhile, there was no way the oil found in the Temple would last that long—but it did. The small quantity of oil burned for eight days, until the messenger returned with new oil suitable for the Menorah. Chanukah celebrates the miracle of the oil.

Purim

The festival of Purim is a happy occasion. It commemorates a historical episode packed with court intrigue, convoluted plots, revelry and insobriety, a cast of characters possessed of every human trait from treachery to jealousy to courage, the near annihilation of the Jewish population, and, finally, its deliverance at the hands of a beautiful damsel.

On Purim, many people arrive to the synagogue in costume or participate in a Purim parade or carnival held at the synagogue. Most often, people dress in costumes representing one of the characters in the Purim story, but contemporary political and historical figures appear as well.

The Story

About 2,500 years after the destruction of the first temple, the Persian king Ahasuerus had married Esther, a beautiful young woman. On the advice of her uncle and guardian, Mordecai, she concealed from him the fact that she was Jewish. Mordecai thwarted a plot to assassinate the king but went unrewarded.

Meanwhile, an evil counselor of the king, Haman, decided to destroy the Jews. He arranged with the king to have them slaughtered on a day that was determined by drawing lots (*purim*). Mordecai learned of the plot and asked Esther to intervene with the king. When Esther did so, Ahasuerus relented. Rather than killing the Jews, he hung Haman from the very gallows the counselor had erected to execute Mordecai.

The day before Purim, the thirteenth of *Adar* (when the story says the massacre of the Jews had been planned), the Jews observe the Fast of Esther, which commemorates her three-day fast before walking in unannounced to confront King Ahasuerus. Like all days of fasting, other than Yom Kippur and Tisha B'Av, the fast lasts from dawn until nightfall.

Haman's Hat

One of the traditional foods eaten at Purim is a small three-sided pastry, called *hamantashen* or Haman's Hat, commemorating the king's evil advisor.

Passover

Passover celebrates the Exodus of the Jews from Egypt, perhaps the most pre-eminent event in Jewish history. Today, Passover remains the most widely observed Jewish holiday.

During their time in Egypt, the Israelites fell out of favor with the Pharaoh. Their growing numbers threatened his power structure.

In an effort to keep the Israelite population in check, the Egyptians enslaved the Hebrews, assigning them harsh work under cruel conditions. Things became even more precarious when Pharaoh was informed by astrologers that an Israelite male child born at that time would grow up to overthrow him. As a result, Pharaoh decreed that every Israelite male newborn be drowned in the Nile River.

Not willing to accept the decree, Amram and Yochebed placed their baby boy in a basket and floated him down the Nile. The boy's sister, Miriam, following at a safe distance, saw the Pharaoh's daughter, Bityah, lift the basket from the river. Bityah called the baby boy Moses.

Moses and the Exodus

Moses grew up as a prince in Pharaoh's palace. One day, he saw an Egyptian overseer striking a Hebrew slave. When the overseer would not stop the beating, Moses killed him. Fearing for his life, Moses fled to Midian, where he became a shepherd and was content with his life until one day, when he was tending to his flock and came upon a burning bush that was not consumed by the flames. It was then that God spoke to Moses, instructing His reluctant emissary to go into Egypt and tell the Pharaoh to let the Israelites leave.

Along with his brother Aaron, Moses conveyed God's demand to Pharaoh, but Pharaoh was angered and only made things worse for the Hebrews. To demonstrate the power of God, ten plagues were visited upon the Egyptians. Before subjecting the Egyptians to the final plague, the slaying of the firstborn males, God directed Moses to instruct each Israelite family to slaughter an unblemished lamb before sundown. They were to smear the blood of the lamb on doorposts and thresholds and then prepare the lamb for their dinner.

During this meal, the Israelites ate the roasted lamb, unleavened bread (because there was not sufficient time for the dough to rise), and *maror* (bitter herbs). While they recounted the many miracles God had performed for them, God passed through Egypt, slaying every firstborn male. Because the houses with the smeared blood of the sacrificial lambs denoting the homes of the Israelites were passed over, the holiday that celebrates the Jews' eventual liberation from Egypt is known as Passover.

What's It Mean?

The Hebrew word for Passover is *Pesach*, derived from the Hebrew root *peh-samech-chet*, which means to pass through or over, or to spare.

The following day, Pharaoh ordered the Israelites to immediately leave Egypt. Under the leadership of Moses, somewhere between 2 and 3 million Israelites departed from Egypt.

Pharaoh soon regretted his decision. He sent his army to pursue the Israelites, catching up with them at the Sea of Reeds. With the sea directly ahead of them and Pharaoh's mighty army at their backs, the Israelites were trapped, but God parted the water and allowed the Israelites to pass through. When the Egyptian army pursued, the water fell back and they all drowned.

Reed Sea or Red Sea

Historical opinion generally agrees that the crossing took place at Lake Timsah, a shallow salt-water lake filled with reeds (hence the name Sea of Reeds). Later narrators moved the site of the crossing to the much deeper Red Sea, making the story a much more dramatic demonstration of God's power.

JEWISH CULTURE

The Ties That Bind All Jews Together

Jews share more than Judaism, their religion. They also have a common culture.

Given a history of almost 4,000 years and the geographic dispersal that forced the Jews to confront and sometimes assimilate other world cultures, Jewish culture has always been heterogeneous. Yet somehow all the diverse customs and practices have managed to come together in a remarkable synthesis.

Jewish Literature

Wherever Jews live in respectable numbers, there is a presence of Jewish literature that augments a sense of oneness as a people. In the last fifty years, American Jewish literature has flourished.

Jewish American Writers

A variety of well-established Jewish American writers have achieved critical acclaim, including Saul Bellow, Henry Roth, Bernard Malamud, Philip Roth, Joseph Heller, Elie Wiesel, Chaim Potok, Cynthia Ozick, and Leon Uris. With young writers of fiction such as Michael Chabon, Myla Goldberg, Thane Rosenbaum, and Allegra Goodman, the future of Jewish literature in twenty-first-century America is secure.

In Israel, not only have Israeli novelists had a great impact on Israelis, but much of their work has been translated from Hebrew, making them accessible to Jewish communities around the globe. We have been fortunate to witness the likes of Aharon Appelfeld, S.Y. Agnon, A.B. Yehoshua, and Amos Oz, as well as the emergence of a new generation of gifted Israeli writers such as David Grossman and Etgar Keret.

Jewish Music

How can you not sense the bond with Jews living in Israel when the resonance of *"Ha-Tikvah"* (the Israeli anthem) fills your ears? And when hearing "Jerusalem of Gold," do you not find yourself closing your eyes and seeing before you the hills of Jerusalem? Nor do you need to understand a word of Yiddish in order to perceive a kinship with all the sons and daughters who ever sang "My Yiddish Momme."

Today there is a resurgence of Jewish music called Klezmer music, reminiscent of the times when groups of itinerant musicians went from village to village in Eastern Europe, entertaining the local Jewish populace with folk songs and folk dance as well as traditional music. Another branch of Jewish music is comprised of traditional and contemporary songs in Hebrew that originate from Israel.

Jewish Food

Food plays an important part in many cultures, and the Jews are no exception in this regard. In fact, food has probably had a greater role in keeping the Jews together as a people than it has for most other groups because food frequently serves both ethnic and religious functions.

Jewish food as a concept is really an amalgamation of many cultures. It reflects the numerous places the Jews have lived over the centuries. Therefore, you will find the influence of Middle Eastern,

Spanish, German, Mediterranean, and Eastern European styles of cooking in Jewish cuisine.

Jewish Food...or Not?

Many foods that you might consider "Jewish" are not exclusive to Jewish cuisine. For example, hummus and falafel are common in much of the Middle East; stuffed cabbage is not just a Jewish food but is prevalent in Eastern Europe; and knishes are familiar to Germans as well as to Jews. Nonetheless, in part because the style of preparation and cooking had to conform with *kashrut* (dietary laws) and in part out of a desire to be original, a Jewish flair and distinct touch was often applied to the foods and cooking techniques extracted from the lands in which Jews resided.

Certain Jewish foods are associated with particular holidays because they are generally served on specific occasions. Of course, there is nothing wrong in having these dishes served throughout the year, which many people choose to do. For instance, Jews serve *challah*, a soft, sweet, eggy bread, as part of the *Shabbat* dinner, as well as at most other festive meals.

What's It Mean?

The word *challah* refers to the portion of dough that was set aside as "the priest's [*kohein's*] share" (Numbers 15:20 and Ezekiel 44:30). When challah is baked, a small piece is customarily tossed into the oven or fire as a token and remembrance of this practice.

Matzah is a flat bread made of a simple mix of flour and water (without any eggs). Food dishes made with matzah abound. One good example is matzah ball soup, which is made of chicken broth with vegetables, like celery and carrots, and matzah balls that are floating in it. These matzah balls are known as *knaydelach* (Yiddish for "dumplings").

Some people like matzah soaked in water and egg and then fried. There is even a Passover variation of latkes (which, by the way, are served on Chanukah) that are made out of matzah meal.

The bagel is a lonely roll to eat all by yourself, because in order for the true taste to come out you need your family.
—Gertrude Berg, actress

Arguably the most quintessentially Jewish food item is the bagel, a donut-shaped piece of bread that is boiled and then baked. Bagels are often topped with sesame seeds or poppy seeds or given a touch of flavor with other ingredients. The addition of cream cheese and lox is a custom born in America.

Bagels for Babies

The first printed reference to the bagel can be found in the Community Regulations of Cracow, Poland, in 1610. At that time, it was the custom to give bagels as a gift to pregnant women shortly before childbirth.

Another popular food item is the blintz. Looking a bit like an egg roll, a blintz is a flat pancake rolled around sweetened cottage cheese, mashed potatoes, jam, or fresh fruit. Blintzes are frequently accompanied with sour cream or applesauce.

Other common Jewish food items include:

- Borscht. Borscht is beet soup, served either hot or cold.
- Knishes. A knish is a potato and flour dumpling normally stuffed with mashed potato and onion, chopped liver, or cheese.
- Kasha. *Kasha* or *kasha varnishkes* is a mixture of buckwheat and bow-tie macaroni noodles.
- Kugel. Kugel is either served as a casserole of potatoes, eggs, and onions or as a dessert made with noodles, fruits, and nuts in an egg-based pudding.
- Kishkas. Parchment paper or plastic filled with either meat or celery and carrots, onions, flour, and spices.
- Gefilte fish. Originally, gefilte fish was stuffed fish, but today it looks more like fish cakes or fish loaf. Gefilte fish may be made from a variety of fish, though it's most often made of carp. The fish is chopped or ground, then mixed with eggs, salt, onions, and pepper, or a vegetable mix.
- Stuffed cabbage. You can prepare stuffed cabbage in a number of ways, one of which is to fill it with beef and then serve in a sweet-and-sour sauce.

ABULAFIA

Father of the Mystical Tradition

Abraham Abulafia (1240–1291) is by far the most influential Kabbalist in the school of Ecstatic (or Prophetic) Kabbalah. In fact, he essentially founded this kabbalistic orientation. His personality was powerful, his ideas were radical and controversial, and his influence has been long lasting.

Abulafia was born in Saragossa, Spain. He spent his first twenty years in Spain before beginning a life that was often characterized by wandering. His rabbinical education was good, but far from outstanding. On the other hand, his knowledge of philosophy was quite extensive.

Abulafia's father died when Abraham was only eighteen, and two years later, he journeyed to the land of Israel in search of the mythical river Sambatyon, beyond which, according to legend, the Ten Lost Tribes of Israel dwelled. From Israel he took a boat from Acco to Greece and spent the next ten years in Greece and Italy. Scholars speculate as to whether he made contact with Sufis (Islamic mystics) in the Land of Israel because some of his meditational methods seemed comparable to those of Sufis. Abulafia also focused on breathing techniques during meditation and scholars wonder whether he may have been indirectly influenced by Yoga via Sufism.

In 1271, at the age of thirty-one, Abulafia had his first transformative experience. He understood the experience as that of attaining prophetic inspiration and he began teaching his methods and insights to a small number of chosen students.

Prolific Author

Abulafia wrote close to fifty works. A little more than half were kabbalistic texts of various sorts. In addition to commentaries on *Sefer Yetzirah* (*The Book of Creation*) and the Jewish philosopher Maimonides's *Moreh Nevukhim* (*Guide for the Perplexed*), he wrote numerous books in which he explains his meditation techniques, teaches the secrets of the various names of God, and writes his insights into the Torah and the *mitzvot* (commandments).

Abulafia also wrote another type of work, which he called his prophetic books. Of the more than twenty that he wrote, only one has survived, *Sefer HaOt* (*The Book of the Sign*; the word *Ot*, however, also means "letter"). These emerge more out of his immediate experiences.

Going to See the Pope

In the summer of 1280, Abulafia went to Rome to see Pope Nicholas III, to speak on behalf of the Jewish people and to persuade the pope to improve the difficult conditions under which they lived. Nicholas, however, was suspicious of him and ordered him arrested and put to death by burning. However, the night of his arrest the pope suddenly died. Abulafia was kept for a month in the College of the Franciscans and was subsequently freed.

After his release, Abulafia went to Sicily and remained there for most of the rest of his life. During this period of time he composed the majority of his books. Abulafia believed that his meditative use of the Hebrew language could give you a deeper understanding of reality than philosophy could. Contemplating the letters and meditating with them would unlock secrets inaccessible by any other means. To Abulafia, the structure of the Hebrew language itself contained within it the secrets of the natural universe.

Functions of the Hebrew Language

For Abulafia, language had two essential functions. The conventional one was communication of our thoughts. The second function was for the attainment of prophecy. Hebrew was believed to be the original language, the language in which Adam named all the animals, the language through which Creation came about. All other languages were understood as in some way coming from it. Another belief was that there were seventy languages. In ancient times, some people took this literally, but by medieval times it was seen as a reference to all the other languages and to all knowledge that humans possess collectively.

Those, like Abulafia, who philosophized about human language in general, tended to think that language came about through human convention, but that Hebrew, the language of divine revelation, reflected reality on a different level. Some saw it as a revealed language, others as a language whose nature made it the ideal medium for communicating revelation.

The Kabbalistic Meaning of Letters

Abulafia wrote that different aspects of the Hebrew alphabet were filled with mystical meaning. The shapes of the letters themselves were not a matter of human convention, but were provided through prophetic insight by those who communicated God's revelation. The names of the letters were deeply significant. The first letter of the Hebrew alphabet, the aleph, for example, is spelled *aleph, lamed, pheh*. The name of the aleph, therefore, has the gematria (a form of biblical interpretation in which each Hebrew letter has a numerical value) of 111, which emphasizes its standing for "unity" (the gematria of the aleph itself is 1). In addition to the visual form and the names of the letters both being meaningful, the numerical equivalents of the letters were highly significant.

Abulafia saw the combining of letters as the construction of something, much as any living being is put together with different parts of the body. *Sefer HaBahir* had said that the vowels were the souls of words and Abulafia agreed with this perspective. The vowels provided various pronunciations of YHVH when using them as a meditation technique with this name. Also, the vowels indicated the head movements and breathing exercises that Abulafia practiced to accompany the pronunciation and meditation on the divine letters.

Permutations of the Divine Names

There are many elements to Abulafia's techniques of letter combinations. He primarily worked with YHVH and with the seventy-two-letter name of God. When using YHVH, he combined each letter individually with the aleph and used five different Hebrew vowels (according to Sephardic Hebrew grammar) in changing combinations. So he might begin with aleph and yud and vocalize them with the same vowel and then proceed with different combinations from there. The vowels he used are the *kholam* (pronounced *oh*), *kamatz* (pronounced *ah*), *khirik* (pronounced *ee*), *tzereh* (pronounced *eh*), and *kubutz* (pronounced *oo*). With great care and concentration, Abulafia put each set of letters together with every possible combination of vowels.

Abulafia saw the divine name as reflecting the structure of reality and also as being embedded in a person's soul. The manipulation of the letters and vowels of the name would consequently change a person's soul and consciousness. Therefore it was especially important that a person undertake these processes with maximum awareness, to avoid causing harm to oneself.

CHAPTER 3

TAOISM AND CONFUCIANISM

Confucianism is not officially considered a world religion because it is not organized as such. It is often grouped with religions, however, perhaps because it is a spiritual philosophy, a social ethic, a political ideology, and a scholarly tradition.

The belief system began in China around the sixth to fifth century B.C. by Confucius. It has been followed by the Chinese people for over two millennia. A major part of the belief is its emphasis on learning; Confucianism is also a source of values. Its influence has spread to many other countries, including Korea, Japan, and Vietnam. Confucianism made its mark extensively in Chinese literature, education, culture, and both spiritual and political life.

Taoism arose in the first century A.D. The name came from the Chinese character that means path or way: Tao. In English it is pronounced "dow." The Tao is a natural force that makes the universe the way it is.

Taoism advocates the philosophy of disharmony or harmony of opposites, meaning there is no love without hate, no light without dark, no male without female—in other words, yin and yang. Collectively the writings called *Tao Tsang* are concerned with the ritual meditations of the Tao.

Taoist thought permeated the Chinese culture in the same way that Confucianism did, and the two are often linked. Taoism became more popular than Confucianism, even though Confucianism had state patronage. Taoism was based on the individual and tended to reject the organized society of Confucianism. The traditions became so well entrenched within China that many people accepted both of them, although they applied the concepts to their lives in different ways.

Taoism was first conceived as a philosophy and evolved into a religion that has a number of deities. Lao-tzu (or Laozi), whom many believed was the founder of Taoism, was so revered that he was thought of as a deity. On the other hand, there were some who thought of him as a mystical character.

A key Taoist concept is that of nonaction or the natural course of things. It is a direct link to yin and yang. Yin (dark/female) represents cold, feminine, evil, and negative principles. The yang (light/male) represents good, masculine, warmth, and positive principles. Yin (the dark side) is the breath that formed the earth. Yang (the light side) is the breath that formed the heavens. Yin and yang are not polar opposites; they are values in people that depend on individual circumstances. So, what is cold for one person may be warm for another. Yin and yang are said to be identical aspects of the same reality.

The study, practice, and readings of yin and yang have become a school of philosophy in its own right. The idea is for the student to find balance in life where yin represents inactivity, rest, and reflection, while yang represents activity and creativity. The basic feature of Taoism is to restore balance. Extremes produce a swinging back to the opposite. Therefore, there is a constant movement from activity to inactivity and back again.

TAOIST WRITINGS

Accept What Is

The major piece of literature in Taoism is Laozi's *Dao de Jing* (*Classic Way of Power*—*de* means power, the energy of Tao at work in the world). It has never been established that Laozi was the sole author. There are no references in the work to other persons, events, places, or even writings that could provide any evidence to assist in placing or dating the composition. The fact that the work can't be authenticated as to its author or place is, again, somehow in keeping with the philosophy of Taoism; the work exists and that is everything.

The essence of the book is pure simplicity: accept what is without wanting to change it. Study the natural order and go with it, rather than against it. The effort to change something creates resistance. Everything nature provides is free; a person should emulate nature and consider everyone as an equal.

> *Be content with what you have; rejoice in the way things are.*
> *When you realize there is nothing lacking,*
> *the whole world belongs to you.*
> —Laozi

If people stand and observe, they will see that work proceeds best if they stop trying too hard. The more extra effort you exert and the harder you look for results, the less gets done. The philosophy of Taoism is to simply be.

The *Dao de Jing* was compiled in an environment that was racked by widespread disorder, wanton self-seeking rulers, and rampant immoral behavior. The popularity of the work has been, and is, widespread. An amazing number of translations have been produced, more than for any other literary work except the Bible. There have been eighty English translations alone.

Feng Shui

One example of the use of harmony and meditation is the practice of Feng Shui. The literal meaning of *Feng Shui* is "wind and water," which are the natural elements that shape the landscape. A Feng Shui expert can advise on how to get the best results in a home or office by establishing the most advantageous alignment of space and furnishings to allow the most positive and harmonious flow of *chi* (energy).

Zhuangzi (fourth century B.C.) was a great Taoist sage. He is best known for the book that bears his name, the *Zhuangzi*, also known as *Nánhuá Zhēnjīng* (*The Pure Classic of Nan-hua*). It is thought to have originally comprised thirty-three chapters, although there may have been more. Again, as it seems with most works of written religious antiquity, there is controversy over what the author wrote and what others contributed. However, scholars agree that the first seven chapters of the *Zhuangzi* were written by the author alone.

He wrote other books highly critical of Confucianism. On the other hand he was seen as being a great influence on the development of Chinese Buddhism. Buddhist scholars considered Zhuangzi to be the primary source for Taoist thought and they drew heavily from his teachings. Overall he was considered the most significant and comprehensive of the Taoist writers.

He lived around 327 B.C., which made him a contemporary of the eminent Confucian scholar, Mencius. All of this confirms yet again how intertwined Taoism, Buddhism, and Confucianism were with each other.

TAOIST RITUALS AND FESTIVALS

Dragons, Ghosts, and the Moon

The religious aspects of Taoism are related more to shamanism than worship in the typical way. Taoist priests usually look after temples in urban areas. Monks and nuns live in temples located in sacred mountains. China has many sacred mountains and some of the temples are even dramatically suspended on the side of them. In general, monks and nuns are permitted to marry. Their work is ensuring the worship of the sacred texts, of which there are some 1,440 books.

In Taoism there is a strong element of the ways and means of achieving immortality. Throughout life, adherents study and practice exercises designed to increase the flow of chi energy, and some will become expert in meditation to the point where they become one with the Tao. A quote from the *Zhuangzi* provides a good clue to the Taoist attitude toward life and death:

> *Birth is not a beginning; death is not an end. There is existence without limitation; there is continuity without a starting point.*

> *Existence without limitation is space. Continuity without a starting point is time. There is birth, there is death, there is issuing forth, there is entering in. That through which one passes in and out without seeing its form, that is the Portal of God.*

Birth and Death

Birth is a time for casting horoscopes. A month after the birth a naming ceremony is held. Death combines elements of Taoism, Buddhism, and Confucianism in regard to life after death. Funeral rites have to be performed correctly in order that the dead join the family ancestors. There is a belief that the soul is judged by the King of Hell. After the body is buried, paper models of money, houses, and cars are burnt to help the soul in the afterlife, perhaps by paying for a release from the King of Hell. After about ten years the body is dug up. The bones are cleaned then reburied at a site often chosen by a Feng Shui expert.

Religion 101 Question

When a Taoist funeral procession passes through the streets on its way to the cemetery, what color do the family and friends of the deceased wear?

White, the traditional color of mourning in China.

Taoist Festivals

Taoists and Buddhists share four major Chinese festivals. In addition, the Taoists have many others throughout the year including the Taoist vegetarian and fasting days.

Chinese New Year

Chinese New Year is the major festival, which is also known as the "Spring Festival." It is a time of great excitement and joy. It is also a time of wonderful and copious food and of gifts and roving bands of musicians that parade through the streets. Families reunite and give lavish gifts to children. Traditionally it is the time when new paper statues of the kitchen god are put up in houses. The door gods, who defend the house against evil spirits, are also replaced with new ones and good luck sayings are hung over the doorways.

The high point of the season is New Year's Eve, when every member of every family returns home. A sumptuous dinner is served, and children receive gifts of red envelopes that contain gifts of lucky money. Firecrackers and whistling rockets seem to be everywhere.

In preparation for the events, every house is thoroughly cleaned so that the New Year will start off fresh and clean. Hair must be cleaned and set prior to the holiday, otherwise a financial setback would be invited. Debts should also be settled so that the coming year can start off with a clean slate.

Following various religious ceremonies, the eleventh day is a time for inviting in-laws to dine. The Lantern Festival, on the fifteenth day after New Year, marks the end of the New Year season.

The Dragon Boat Festival

The Dragon Boat Festival is celebrated with boats in the shape of dragons. Competing teams row their boats forward to a drumbeat in an effort to win the race. Celebrated in June, the festival has two stories about the history of its meaning. The first one is about the watery suicide of an honest young official who tried to shock the emperor into being kinder to the poor. The race commemorates the people's attempt to rescue the boy in the lake from the dragons who rose to eat him. It is looked at as a celebration of honest government and physical strength.

The other story says the boats race to commemorate the drowning of a poet on the fifth day of the fifth lunar month in 277 B.C. Citizens throw bamboo leaves filled with cooked rice into the water so the fish can eat it rather than the hero poet.

Hungry Ghosts Festival

The third great festival is the Hungry Ghosts Festival. Taoists and Buddhists believe that the souls of the dead imprisoned in hell are freed during the seventh month, when the gates of hell are opened. The released souls are permitted to enjoy feasts that had been prepared for them so that they would be pacified and would do no harm. Offerings and devotions, too, are made to please these ghosts and even musical events are staged to entertain them.

Mid-Autumn Festival

The Mid-Autumn Festival is also called the Moon Festival because of the bright harvest moon, which appears on the fifteenth day of the eighth lunar month. The round shape of the moon means family reunion, so, naturally, the holiday is particularly important for members of a family.

One myth says that on the moon were the fairy Chang E, a woodcutter named Wu Gang, and a jade rabbit that was Chang E's pet. In the old days people paid respect to the fairy Chang E and her pet. The custom has gone now, but moon cakes are sold during the month before the arrival of the Moon Festival.

Another story concerns the goddess Sheng O, whose husband discovered the pill of immortality and was about to eat it and become a cruel ruler for eternity. Sheng O swallowed the pill instead, but the Gods saved her and transported her to the moon. She lives there to this day.

THE TEACHINGS OF CONFUCIUS

The Search for Order

Confucius lived in a time of political violence, so the stage was set for a teacher to emerge who had the ability to dispense a spiritual philosophy that would generate restorative thoughts of social and ethical calm, and who saw perfection in all people. It has been said that he initially attracted more than 3,000 students, some of whom became close disciples.

Confucius was born in the small state of Lu in 552 B.C., in what is now Shantung Province. *Confucius* is a Latin version of *Kong Fuzi* (Kong the master). He was born into an aristocratic family that had seen much better times. His father died when he was only three years old. His mother educated him at home. By the time he was a teenager, he inquired about everything and had set his heart on learning.

He started off as a keeper of stores and accounts, but moved on to other minor posts in government. However, he had difficulty in finding a good job even though he was ambitious and willing to do more or less anything. But, he never gave up his first love: learning. He found teachers who would school him in music, archery, calligraphy, and arithmetic. From his family he had learned the classics: poetry, literature, and history.

When he was nineteen years of age he married a woman of a similar background to his own. Not much else is known about her. They apparently had a son and a daughter.

Confucius the Teacher

All the learning Confucius had done qualified him to teach, which he started to do in his thirties. He was the first person to devote his whole life to learning and teaching for the sole purpose of trying to improve the lot of his fellow humans. He also became known as the first teacher in China whose concern was providing education for all. The rich had tutors for their children. He believed that everyone could benefit from self-education. During his life he worked to open the doors of education to everyone, and he defined learning as not only the acquisition of knowledge but also the building of character.

A major thrust in his teaching was filial piety, the virtue of devotion to one's parents. He considered it the foundation of virtue and the root of human character.

Interestingly, the male attitude toward sex was strict. The purpose of sex was to conceive children, in particular sons. According to Dr. Mel Thompson, an authority in eastern philosophy, there is a sense that male energy is dissipated through sexual union, and that men may be worn out both physically and morally by too much sex. Sexual excess on the part of a ruler was given as a valid reason to take from him the right to rule.

Proper social behavior and etiquette were considered essential to right living. A set of ethics is contained in the *Analects*, a collection of moral and social teachings, which amount to a code of human conduct. Many of the sayings were passed on orally. Here are some examples:

> *Clever words and a plausible appearance have seldom turned out to be humane.*

Young men should be filial when at home and respectful to elders when away from home. They should be earnest and trustworthy. Although they should love the multitude far and wide, they should be intimate only with the humane. If they have any energy to spare after so doing, they should use it to study culture.

The gentleman is calm and peaceful; the small man is always emotional.

The gentleman is dignified but not arrogant. The small man is arrogant but not dignified.

In his attitude to the world the gentleman has no antagonisms and no favoritisms. What is right he sides with.

If one acts with a view to profit, there will be much resentment.

One who can bring about the practice of five things everywhere under Heaven has achieved humaneness . . . Courtesy, tolerance, good faith, diligence, and kindness.

Jen

Confucius concentrated his teachings on his vision, *Jen*, which has been translated in the most complete way as: love, goodness, and human-heartedness; moral achievement and excellence in character; loyalty to one's true nature, then righteousness, and, finally, filial piety. All this adds up to the principle of virtue within the person.

Growth of His Reputation

Around age fifty a turning point came in Confucius's life. He was given an important job and was asked his advice about how to induce the people to be loyal. He answered, "Approach them with dignity, and they will respect you. Show piety towards your parents and kindness toward your children, and they will be loyal to you. Promote those who are worthy, train those who are incompetent; that is the best form of encouragement."

The reputation of Confucius grew, as did the number of his disciples. Trouble came, of course, because he generated the enmity of those who opposed his teachings and growing influence. His political career was short-lived, and at the age of fifty-six when he realized his influence had declined, he moved on and tried to find a feudal state in which he could teach and give service. He was more or less in exile, but his reputation as a man of virtue spread.

When he was sixty-seven years old he returned home to teach, write, and edit. He died in 479 B.C. at the age of seventy-three.

CONFUCIAN LITERATURE AND RITUALS

Birth, Marriage, Death, and Beyond

The most important Confucian literature comprises two sets of books. The major one is the Five Classics. While Confucius may not have personally written them, he certainly was associated with them. The Five Classics contain five visions:

1. *I Ching (Classic of Changes)*
2. *Shu Ching (Classic of History)*
3. *Shih Ching (Classic of Poetry)*
4. *LiChi (Collection of Rituals)*
5. *Ch'un-ch'iu (Spring and Autumn Annals)*

For 2,000 years their influence has been without parallel in the history of China.

When Chinese students were studying for civil service examinations between 1313 and 1905, they were required to study the Five Classics. However, before they reached that level, they tackled the Four Books, which served as an introduction to the Five. The Four Books are:

1. *Great Learning*
2. *Doctrine of the Mean*
3. *Analects*
4. *Mencius*

Of these texts, only the *Analects* contains anything reputedly written by Confucius himself. The Four Books have commentaries by Zhu Xi (1130–1200), a great Neo-Confucian philosopher who helped revitalize Confucianism in China. Confucian Classics, as they were called, became the core curriculum for all levels of education.

The *I Ching*

The *I Ching*, one of the Five Classics of Confucianism, combines divinatory art with numerological techniques and ethical insight. Accordingly there are said to be two complementary and conflicting vital energies: yin and yang. Enthusiasts have claimed that this Classic of Changes is a means of understanding, and even controlling, future events.

Rituals and Customs

As Confucianism does not have all the elements of a religion, and is primarily an ethical movement, it lacks sacraments and liturgy. However, the rituals that occur at important times in a person's life became part of the movement. Confucianism recognizes and regulates four life passages—birth, reaching maturity, marriage, and death. At the root is the ritual of respect: A person must exhibit respect to gain respect.

Birth: The Tai-shen (spirit of the fetus) protects the expectant woman and deals harshly with anyone who harasses the mother-to-be. The mother is given a special diet and is allowed to rest for a month after delivery. The mother's family is responsible for coming up with all that is required by the baby on the first-, fourth-, and twelfth-month anniversaries of the birth.

Marriage: A couple goes through six stages in the marriage process:

1. *Proposal.* The couple exchanges the year, month, day, and hour of each of their births. If any unpropitious event happens within the bride-to-be's family during the following three days, then the woman is believed to have rejected the proposal.
2. *Engagement.* After the wedding day has been chosen, the bride announces the wedding with invitations and a gift of cookies made in the shape of the moon.
3. *Dowry.* This is carried to the groom's home in a solemn procession. Gifts by the groom to the bride, equal in value to the dowry, are sent to her.
4. *Procession.* The groom visits the bride's home and brings her back to his place, with much fanfare.
5. *Marriage and reception.* The couple recite their vows that bond them together for a lifetime, toast each other with wine, then take center stage at a banquet.
6. *Morning after.* The bride serves breakfast to the groom's parents, who then reciprocate.

Death: At death, the relatives cry aloud to inform the neighbors. The family starts mourning and puts on clothes made of coarse material. The corpse is washed and placed in a coffin. Mourners bring incense and money to offset the cost of the funeral. Food and significant objects of the deceased are placed into the coffin. A Buddhist or Taoist priest, or even a Christian minister, performs the burial ritual. Friends and family follow the coffin to the cemetery, each bearing a willow branch, which symbolizes the soul of the person who has died. The branch is later carried back to the family altar where it is used to "install" the spirit of the deceased. Liturgies are performed on the seventh, ninth, and forty-ninth day after the burial, and on the first and third anniversaries of the death.

Spread of Confucianism

On Confucius's death his students compiled his thoughts in *Spring and Autumn Annals*. Mencius spread the values of Confucianism throughout the known world. With the increasing popularity of Confucius, his disciples and followers left sacrifices in temples dedicated to him.

LAOZI

Founder of Taoism

Relatively little reliable information is known about Laozi—surprising, given the immense influence his philosophy of Taoism has had. He probably lived during the sixth century B.C., although it's possible he lived a century or so earlier. He may (or may not) have been a contemporary of Confucius. Supposedly he was born in the village of Chu Jen.

Myths and legends have grown up about him over the centuries. According to one, his mother conceived him while gazing at a falling star and gave birth to him after bearing him in her womb for sixty-two years. He emerged (not surprisingly, after that length of time) with a long full gray beard. He lived, according to another tradition, for 999 years.

Tradition says he was a keeper of archives in the royal bureaucracy of the Zhou dynasty and was a scholar. Like many of the philosophers of ancient Greece, he never founded a formal school but instead gathered around himself a group of students, whom he taught by both speech and example. Although there are accounts of his meeting with Confucius and debates between the two men, most scholars agree that these are probably false and are merely anti-Confucian propaganda put out by Taoists.

Among his disciples was one Yinxi, to whom he dictated the text of the *Tao-de Ching*. Yinxi became a follower of the sage when Laozi, tired of the corruption and materialism of men, walked into the west, intending to live as a hermit. Yinxi was a guard at the western gate of the kingdom and recognized Laozi. He asked to be taught by the master, explaining that he had made a detailed study of astrology, which allowed him to recognize the portents of the master's approach.

Yinxi was put hard to the test by Laozi, and after many years of study, endeavoring to find his Tao, Laozi elevated him and took him on a journey through the entire universe. The relationship of the two men is taken as an exemplar of the ideal relationship between master and student.

Laozi's Philosophy

The Taoist philosophy can perhaps be best summed up in a quote from Zhuang Zhou (Zhuangzi): *"To regard the fundamental as the essence, to regard things as coarse, to regard accumulation as deficiency, and to dwell quietly alone with the spiritual and the intelligent—herein lie the techniques of Tao of the ancients."*

CHAPTER 4
CHRISTIANITY

Christianity refers to many religious traditions that have grown from a single source. These include Catholicism, Protestantism (which itself has many divisions), Copts, Eastern Orthodox Christianity, and countless small sects. What all of them have in common is the teachings of Jesus Christ as they have evolved over the past 2,000 years. Christianity has had an incalculable effect on the world, both on its culture and language, and on its political and social development. There are churches and cathedrals in every city and town (practically on every street corner). Western governments have established national holidays around Christian rituals, and we live by a calendar that measures time according to "Before Christ" and "Anno Domini" (in the year of Our Lord).

Christianity is also one of three religions (the other two are Judaism and Islam) that exist within what's called the "Abrahamic tradition," that is, they trace elements of their beliefs to Abraham, father of Isaac and chosen by God as the father of nations. Abraham's story is among the most moving episodes of the Old Testament and has provided grist for innumerable scholars and exegetes over the centuries. But the specifically Christian tradition begins with the coming of Jesus of Nazareth.

JESUS OF NAZARETH

The Man and the Christ

What we know about Jesus comes from the four gospels written by Mark, Matthew, Luke, and John (mostly from the first three, known as the Synoptic Gospels). None of the gospel writers were contemporaries of Jesus, so a lot of details about him are murky. In fact, he's probably the greatest world-historical figure about whom the least is known.

According to tradition, he was born in humble circumstances: son of a carpenter, born in a stable as his parents Joseph and Mary journeyed to Bethlehem to take part in the Roman census.

December? Try June!

Although Christians celebrate Christ's birth on December 25, nothing in the Bible supports this as his birthday. Since he was born around the time of the census, it's possible he may have been born as late as June, a traditional time for the census. Some scholars place his birthday in September or March. To make things even more complicated, scholars have concluded that he was born about five years earlier than the beginning of the current general calendar, or about 5 B.C.

Jesus was Jewish; he was raised in the Jewish tradition under Jewish law. When he reached adulthood, together with a group of his disciples (students), he traveled Palestine to spread the word of God. Jesus' message came from Jewish roots but was also new. He taught that God wanted people to live their lives in goodness, love, and simplicity.

THE TWELVE DISCIPLES	
Simon	Jesus named him *Peter* (Greek) or *Cephus* (Aramaic), which means "rock." He is often considered the leader of the twelve.
Andrew	Simon Peter's brother; he and John were the first disciples Jesus called.
James (son of Zebedee)	John's brother; killed in A.D. 44 by Herod Agrippa I.
John (son of Zebedee)	James's brother.
Philip	Like Peter and Andrew, from Bethsaida.
Thomas	Later called "Doubting Thomas" because when Jesus appeared to the disciples after his resurrection, Thomas at first refused to believe it was him.
Bartholomew	One of the disciples to whom Jesus appeared on the sea of Tiberias after his resurrection.
James (son of Alphaeus)	Also known as James the Younger.
Thaddeus	Also known as "Judas, the brother of James."
Simon	Also known as the Zealot; he later evangelized Ethiopia and Persia.
Judas Iscariot	The betrayer of Jesus, he committed suicide after Jesus was condemned to die.
Matthew	One of Jesus' early followers; a tax collector

Miracles and Parables

Jesus performed many miracles, including walking on water across the Sea of Galilee; turning water into wine at a wedding feast at Cana; reviving Lazarus from the dead; and feeding 5,000 hungry people with five loaves of bread and two fishes. The point of these miracles was to build faith among his disciples and show them he had power that could only come from God. Christians also interpret these miracles allegorically: For instance, the food is actually a symbol of spiritual enrichments. Receiving Jesus' spiritual message and accepting knowledge of him is food for the soul.

Jesus also spread his teaching through parables, or stories. Sometimes these are actual stories and sometimes they are metaphors. For instance, in Matthew 13:31–32:

> *"He put before them another parable: 'The kingdom of heaven is like a mustard seed that someone took and sowed in his field; it is the smallest of all the seeds, but when it has grown it is the greatest of shrubs and becomes a tree, so that the birds of the air come and make nests in its branches.'"*

To most theologians' thinking Jesus' message is that faith begins as the smallest seed in the hearts of human beings. When the seed is sown and nurtured, it grows into something bigger, stronger, and more beautiful. To sow the seed is to accept the word of God, which in turn will transform the person from within in the same way the seed is transformed into a plant or a tree.

Before the Pharisees and Sadducees

Jesus' message was a very powerful one, and he also offended conservative groups within the Jewish establishment. These forces, the Pharisees and Sadducees, formed an alliance against Jesus and called for his arrest.

Betrayed by his disciple Judas, Jesus was taken before the Roman governor, Pontius Pilate, tried, and condemned to death by crucifixion. Jesus was crucified on a hill outside Jerusalem. Over his head the Romans inscribed the letters INRI (*Iesus Nazarenus Rex*

Iudaeorum, Jesus of Nazareth, King of the Jews). This was intended to serve as a warning to the Jewish people not to oppose Roman rule.

Factions in the Jewish Hierarchy

- The Pharisees: A group of staunchly restrictive Jewish leaders
- The Sadducees: A conservative political group that represented the aristocracy of the Jewish society
- The Zealots: A group that believed in armed revolt against the Romans
- The Essenes: A group neither politically active nor violent, they took to the wilderness to study religious writings

Resurrection

In the days that followed Jesus' death, his followers felt hopeless. How, they asked one another, could Jesus be the Messiah, the chosen leader who would lead the Jewish people out of captivity? He was gone and the people still lived under the Roman Empire.

Hope was renewed when rumors spread that Jesus had risen from the dead. His tomb was empty, and several people reported they had seen him.

As the apostles celebrated the Jewish Feast of Weeks (*Pentecost* in Greek), the Holy Spirit came among them, and the apostle Peter announced the resurrection to a huge crowd, claiming it had been predicted in the Old Testament. He told the people there assembled to go forth and baptize in the name of the Holy Spirit. So in about A.D. 33, more than 3,000 people were baptized, an event celebrated by some Christians during Pentecost.

EARLY CHRISTIANS

Spreading the Good News

After the crucifixion of Jesus, the twelve apostles were puzzled and afraid. Jesus, they believed, was the Messiah, whose coming had been foretold by prophets and who would free them from Roman rule. Yet now he was dead, and they were not free.

Once, however, they concluded that Jesus had been resurrected, they underwent a radical change. Now Jesus was not just the Jewish Messiah but a savior for all mankind. His death thus became a means by which he redeemed man from Original Sin and promised a glorious new life. The apostles began to preach and spread this good news.

The Gospels

The four gospels that bring to us the news of Jesus Christ's life and teachings are the Gospels of Mark, Matthew, Luke, and John. The four Gospels recount the same story, but each author concentrates on different aspects and a different message:

- The Gospel of Mark (A.D. 65–70) focuses on Jesus' suffering, with which persecuted Christians could identify.
- The Gospel of Matthew (A.D. 80–100) explains how Jesus, as the Messiah, fulfills Jewish prophecies.
- The Gospel of Luke (A.D. 85) points out how Jesus, as Savior, does not discriminate on the basis of race or class.
- The Gospel of John (circa A.D. 90) formulates the difficult notion of Jesus as a divine being.

What's It Mean?

The word *gospel* means "good news." Along with the four gospels that are included in the New Testament, there are many others, though they are not accepted as canonical. They include:

- The Gospel of Thomas
- The Gospel of Marcion
- The Gospel of Mary
- The Gospel of Judas
- The Gospel of the Four Heavenly Realms

Tests of Faith: The Martyrs

The Roman emperors did not appreciate the new religion that rejected their almost-divine status, all other Roman deities, and their religious holidays. (Celebrating these holidays was supposed to bring the gods' favor to Rome, and it was considered patriotic duty; rejection of the gods was therefore considered treason.)

Still, Christians lived in Rome with relative peace until A.D. 64, when a terrible fire swept the city's cramped streets. The causes of the fire remain unknown, but the Emperor Nero blamed the Christians and reprisals followed. Christianity was proclaimed anti-Roman and outlawed around the year 100.

Practicing or preaching Christianity was punishable by death, and yet many early Christians chose to stand behind their beliefs. They preferred to die as martyrs rather than renounce their faith. Their courage and willingness to cling to their faith despite everything impressed the people of Rome. Christianity continued to attract converts and to spread.

The First Martyr

Tradition names Stephen as the first Christian martyr. One year after the Crucifixion, Stephen was preaching to the crowd in Jerusalem. Stephen's speech was so inflammatory—he also accused his listeners of not keeping the law given them by the angels—that he was dragged outside Jerusalem and stoned to death. Later, he was canonized by the Church and became a saint.

The apostles Peter and Paul met their deaths under the Romans. Peter, who had established a Christian community in Rome, was arrested there and sentenced to crucifixion. According to one story, Peter requested to be crucified upside down, so that his death would not reflect that of his Lord.

Why Crucifixion?

Rome adopted crucifixion as a form of punishment from the Persians and used it in the repression of its subjugated peoples. We know from the Roman writer Cicero (106–43 B.C.) that crucifixion was used against slaves and non-Roman citizens, particularly against those who had fomented rebellion or committed other treasonous acts.

Rome Embraces Christianity

For its first 300 years, Christianity was viewed with great suspicion. Christian communities grew, but people joined them at great personal peril. Believers worshiped in secret. Christians were harassed and persecuted throughout the Roman Empire; they had no political power. The empire itself was under stress from without and within. Roman territories were under barbarian attack, while at home the Roman aristocracy was growing weak and corrupt. Under siege and without great leaders, Rome was falling apart.

In 312, the Roman army stationed in Britain elected Constantine (c. 272–337) the next Roman emperor. He returned to Rome, knowing that he would have to fight for his position when he got there. As Constantine prepared for battle at the Milvian Bridge on the River Tiber near Rome, he had a vision of a cross. He took this as a sign and ordered his soldiers to paint the Greek letters for the word "Christ" on their shields. Constantine defeated his rival and entered Rome victorious, as the new emperor. Although he did not convert to Christianity until shortly before his death many years later, both he and Rome officially supported Christianity.

Constantine was the author of the Edict of Milan, which allowed Christians the freedom to worship openly and freely.

Another Roman emperor, Theodosius the Great (346–395), the last emperor to rule both the eastern and western Roman empires, tolerated pagan practices early in his reign. Toward the end of his life, he became much stricter, slowly eroding pagan power and rights to worship, until he passed an edict that outlawed pagan practices altogether.

Theodosius also streamlined the church by suppressing several important heresies, Arianism and Manichaeism, in Constantinople.

What Is a Heresy?

A heresy is a challenge to an accepted belief. Two heresies that arose during the fourth century were Arianism and Manichaeism. Arianism, taught by an Alexandrian priest named Arius, denied Jesus' divinity. According to Arius, Jesus was made by God and is therefore subordinate to God. Manichaeism, a synthesis of different religious systems, taught that one god created good and another evil, and that mortals were not responsible for their sins. Although Arianism was declared heretical and eventually disappeared, for a time a majority of Christians were probably Arians.

The Rise of the Papacy in Rome

In the fourth century, the power of the popes in Rome continued to grow. Pope Damasus I (366–383) as well as those who followed him made the Church more powerful and established the idea that when they spoke a papal utterance, they were speaking through the mouth of Peter. After Rome fell in 410, during the papacy of Innocent I (died 417), the office of the pope moved in to fill the vacuum of leadership.

These popes all wrote about the glory of the Church in Rome, and this is where the formal title, Holy Roman Catholic Church, comes from.

The entire Catholic Church spread over the globe is the sole bridal chamber of Christ. The Church of Rome has been placed above all other churches not by virtue of conciliar decree, but by virtue of the words of the Lord: "Thou art Peter!"
—Damasus, fourth-century pope

MONKS AND MONASTERIES

The Love of Learning and the Desire for God

Right from the early years of Christianity, there were many Christians who wanted to worship in the way they believed Christ meant them to: reflectively, introspectively, with purity of body and mind—and so they did. In most cases, this meant relinquishing their belongings and renouncing their families and past existence for a life of isolation in a place that they felt would bring them spiritually closer to God and the true message of Christ.

Generally, a monk vowed:

1. To live a life of poverty
2. To lead a life of chastity
3. To be obedient to the authority of the monastic order and to God

Hermits

Some monks chose to live apart from society, dwelling in desert caves or other isolated spots. They were often highly educated and from well-born families, so their sacrifice was considerable.

Nuns

The first hermits were actually women, who were known in Latin as *nonnus* or nuns. Later their communities became known as convents. Women often joined convents for reasons other than religious ones: to avoid unwanted marriages, for instance, or to save their fathers the cost of expensive wedding dowries.

Life in a Monastery

Hermits in Western Europe gradually realized that living alone and in isolation might not be what God had in mind for them. They came together to form communities, or monasteries. These monks were known as *cenobites*. Hermits, or *anchorites*, remained a cultural element in Eastern Europe long after the practice had largely died away in the West.

Monks believed that by living simply, they were returning to the original state of grace in which mankind lived before the Fall of Adam and Eve. In a shared community, helping each other, they grew their own crops, tended their own animals, grew their own herbs to make medicines, and eventually even came to manufacture wine and cheese in order to support their way of life.

The Benedictine Rule

Over time, monasteries established various "Rules," or sets of commandments for living within the monastery. Among the oldest and most influential of these is the Benedictine Rule, drawn up by St. Benedict (480–550), an Italian monk. Benedict's rule was not considered to be a book of extremes in the same way other monastic living writings were, but taught a mellow way of living in true devotion to Christ. The rule sought to balance manual labor with study and ritual prayer, as well as mandating poverty, chastity, and obedience. By putting all this into a single manuscript, Benedict was able to outline what he considered the ideal form of monastic living. Benedictine orders of monks exist to this day and still live by the Rule.

Other Monastic Orders

Over the course of the Middle Ages, some devotees came to believe that the Benedictine Order (as those who lived according to the Benedictine Rule were known) had become corrupt. They founded their own orders. Among the most prominent were:

- The Cistercians
- The Carthusians
- The Dominicans
- The Franciscans

Often these orders differentiated from one another by the colors of their robes, or habits. Dominicans, for example, wore black habits, while Franciscans wore brown ones.

Daily Life in a Monastery

A monk's day was regulated by services, or canonical hours. These were:

- Matins (2 A.M.)
- Laudes (5 A.M.)
- Prime (7 A.M.)
- Terce (9 A.M.)
- Sexte (noon)
- Nones (2 P.M.)
- Vespers (4 P.M.)
- Compline (6 P.M.)

In between these services, the monks might be assigned to work in the garden, clean or repair the monastic buildings, accommodate visitors (monasteries were often treated as inns by travelers), or copy manuscripts in the monastery's scriptorium.

Medieval Copyists

Monks in the Middle Ages spent a great deal of time copying manuscripts. Before the invention of the printing press, this was the only way of preserving texts, and the monks regarded it as a sacred charge to copy the gospels and other religious writings. They also copied many manuscripts containing works by ancient authors from Rome and Greece (though countless others were lost). The monks not only copied these works; they illustrated, or *illuminated*, them. Many illuminations were extremely rich in detail and skill and represent one of the major art forms of the Middle Ages. One of the greatest examples of monastic illumination is the Irish *Book of Kells*. You can see samples of it online at *www.digitalcollections.tcd.ie/home/index.php?DRIS_ID=MS58_003v*.

Although many monasteries were the targets of raids by the Northmen beginning in the ninth century, the institution survived, revived, and flourished in the High Middle Ages during the tenth through fourteenth centuries. Thanks to them, Western Europe inherited the rich religious traditions of early Christianity as well as much of the literature, philosophy, and other learning of ancient Greece and Rome.

THE REFORMATION

The Reformation is the name given to a dramatic upheaval within the Catholic Church, which occurred between 1500 and 1625. These are only approximate dates, since there were various church reformers before 1500 and continued reform and conflict after 1625. As early as the fourteenth century, reformers such as John Wyclif (1330–1384) railed against the corruption of the church leadership in Rome. After his death, some of his followers, known as Lollards, continued to spread his message.

The most influential reformer was Martin Luther (1483–1546), which whom the Reformation is most associated. Luther attended the university at Erfurt, aspiring to become a lawyer. However, in 1505 he had a terrifying experience. While traveling from Mansfield to Erfurt, Luther was struck by lightning. As he lay in the road, he prayed to St. Anna, promising that if she helped him survive, he would become a monk. He did survive, and true to his word he entered an Augustinian monastery in Erfurt.

Struggle and Disillusionment

Luther's time at the monastery was unhappy. He began to question the God of the scriptures as well as his own relationship to God. He sought to purge himself from sin through fasting, meditation, and self-flagellation. By 1507, when he was ordained a priest, he wondered if he was really up to such a task. In 1510 he traveled to Rome. He was happy when he got there but his happiness was short-lived. Rome was a city of corruption and materialism with a religiously indifferent population. Luther left a very disillusioned man and continued his studies and teaching in the town of Wittenberg (where he received his doctorate in theology).

To Be ... Or Not to Be?

Decades after Luther's defiance of the papacy, Wittenberg was still highly symbolic of change and turmoil. In *Hamlet*, Shakespeare makes the young prince of Denmark, tortured by indecision and by unaccustomed thoughts, a former student at Wittenberg.

Luther found the core of his answer in St. Paul's letter to the Romans. From this he derived the basic element of his philosophy: People achieve salvation by faith alone. If they believe in God through Christ's sacrifice on the cross, they are absolved of sin and will receive God's grace. This has nothing to do with doing good deeds—donating money to rebuild St. Peter's cathedral in Rome, for example.

In this, Luther attacked a prevalent practice of the church: indulgences. The church raised money for its vast projects by soliciting donations from Christians. In return for these donations, the church granted an indulgence from sin. Luther was offended by this idea, especially as it was practiced by Johann Tetzel (1465–1519). In 1517 Tetzel was on a mission from Rome to raise funds for the rebuilding of St. Peter's basilica. In his preaching, Tetzel promised that the Christians who donated their money to this venture would be given an indulgence, which consisted of granting the pardon for past sins without penance, the release from purgatory of loved ones, and the pardon of sins that have not yet been committed.

Luther attacked this on three points:

1. Only God, not the church, can grant salvation.
2. The church was taking advantage of Christians (especially poor ones) for its own material benefit.
3. A Christian is not automatically given salvation for good works, but a good Christian automatically does good works.

Luther refuted Tetzel's teachings in the form of ninety-five propositions, or "theses." Legend has it (quite possibly incorrectly) that he nailed these to the church door in Wittenberg. In any case, he published them, and they became widely known.

Protestantism and Printing

Many historians argue that one reason Luther's attack on the leadership of the church was so successful was because of a new communications technology then available in Western Europe: the printing press. Johannes Gutenberg (c. 1395–1468) first used movable type to print around 1439. By 1450 he had set up a printing shop. It's notable that the first book he printed was the Bible, printed in an edition of about 180 copies in 1455. Thus the works of Protestants such as Luther could be reproduced in large numbers and distributed throughout Europe.

Luther's ideas continued to evolve during the next few decades. By 1520 Luther had launched a full-scale attack against the church. He argued that:

1. If Christ is the head of the church, what need do Christians have for a pope?
2. The sacraments hold Christians captive of Rome.
3. The only valid sacraments are those instituted by Christ, not those invented by the church.

Luther declared the pope to be the Anti-Christ; the pope, in turn, declared Luther to be a heretic, whose writings were to be burned.

Other Reformers

By this time, the dispute had spread across Europe, where it had social as well as theological impacts. In Germany, peasants wanted to participate in newfound religious freedom, and they also demanded social, political, and economic reform. They formulated twelve demands:

1. Each parish should choose its own pastor.
2. Some forms of tithing (that is, church taxes) should be abolished.
3. Serfdom, the tying of peasants to the land, should be done away with.
4. Peasants should have the right to hunt and fish freely.
5. Peasants should be able to collect building materials and firewood freely from forests.
6. Lords should stop imposing oppressive workloads.
7. Peasants should only work according to what is "just and proper" according to an agreement between lord and peasant.
8. Rents should be affordable.
9. There should be equal justice for lord and peasant.
10. Unfair division of land should be done away with.
11. The death tax should be abolished.

12. If any of these demands did not adhere to the word of God, it would be scrapped.

The princes and rulers of Germany were not about to allow such radical demands to be implemented. The result was a civil war that left more than 100,000 peasants dead. Luther sided with the landowners during the war, with the result that the peasants (especially in the south of Germany) turned their backs on Luther and sided with more radical religious movements.

Religious reform continued to spread throughout Western Europe, aided by such thinkers as Ulrich Zwingli (1484–1531) and John Calvin (1509–1564). Although these men, like many others, came to disagree with Luther, on one point they were agreed: They did not recognize the pope as the head of the church. This became the most basic point of separation between Protestants and Catholics.

MISSIONARIES

Sending God's Glory Through the World

As part of the reaction against the Reformation, the Catholic Church encouraged the formation of a new order of monks, the Society of Jesus, more commonly known as the Jesuits. Founded by a Spanish soldier, Inigo de Loyola (1491–1556), the Jesuits were highly disciplined and militaristic in their organization. This made them an excellent agency with which to spread the teachings of the church throughout the world.

Glory to God!

In the early seventeenth century, there were more than 13,000 Jesuits all over the world. The motto for the Society became *Ad maiorem Dei gloriam*, Latin for "To the greater glory of God!" This reflected the high standards for which they stood.

Loyola developed strict standards for entry into the Society, the most important of which was education. With education, the Jesuits not only believed that they instilled the Catholic doctrine in the areas where they taught, but they saw themselves as preparing to spread it to the rest of the world as well.

The late fifteenth and sixteenth centuries have been dubbed the Age of Discovery. The Jesuits were instrumental in assisting explorers to convert "heathens" across the world. Aboard almost any sailing vessel in this time period was a Jesuit, a Dominican, a Franciscan, or an Augustinian. It was their task to convert the natives in each newly discovered region.

St. Francis Xavier

Francis Xavier (1506–1552) was one of the seven original members of the Society of Jesus and among the most dedicated missionaries ever. Xavier's mission was to convert the population of the Far East. He launched his mission as a papal legate (or messenger) under the commission of Portugal, from the Portuguese seaport of Goa, India. His work in Goa was brief, and feeling he was leaving the port in a state of moral well-being, he set his sights on the remote regions of southern India.

While there, the local village fishermen (Paravars) sought refuge with the Portuguese explorers from invading robbers who were making their lives impossible. The Portuguese agreed to help them if they submitted to baptism and the Christian faith. Out of desperation, the Paravars agreed, but it went no further. They had no idea what Christianity was and no one bothered to teach them until Xavier came. He read to the villagers from scripture and helped them memorize the Ten Commandments, the Apostolic Creed, the Lord's Prayer, and other rituals. Once they had sufficiently consumed the words and the faith behind the words, Xavier baptized them by the hundreds.

On the perimeters of Christendom, however, were the Hindus and the Muslims. While Xavier has been praised for his influence and ambition, he is criticized for his call for an inquisition to convert the Muslims. The king of Portugal agreed, and the "Inquisition" lasted in Goa until the early nineteenth century. In an effort to destroy all signs of heathenism, parts of India were leveled.

The Japanese Experience

In 1538, Xavier arrived in Japan, where the Jesuits left a lasting impression. Eager for change from their feudal system to a world of prosperity and trade, the Japanese welcomed the outsiders. Upon arrival, Xavier was pleased that Buddhism was fading from the psyche of the people.

Japan changed Xavier's thinking about destructive imperialism. He was enamored of Japanese culture, and while he knew they needed to accept scripture and adopt the Christian faith, he believed these could be integrated into the existing lifestyle of the people.

The Jesuits remained in Japan well into the sixteenth century, leaving behind some 300,000 converts and two colleges in the Jesuit-established town of Nagasaki. However, these endeavors died in the seventeenth century when new rulers of foreign nations declared the missionaries to be foreign invaders and launched a policy of Christian persecution. Nagasaki collapsed, and Christianity disintegrated in Japan.

The Chinese Challenge

Xavier died before he could make it to China, and another Jesuit, Matteo Ricci, undertook his missionary work in that nation.

Finding that Confucianism was ensconced in Chinese culture and represented a serious challenge to Christian doctrine, Ricci taught that Christianity was not new in China. Rather, it was a new expression of existing religious beliefs. Instead of bombarding his way with force and wrath, he learned the culture and the language of the region and made attempts to talk to the Chinese leaders, honoring them with gifts and friendship. When Ricci died in 1610, there were 2,000 Christians in China.

The Clocks

Among the gifts Ricci gave the emperor during his stay in Beijing were two clocks. The emperor loved them, but at some point they stopped working. Chinese experts couldn't figure out how to get them working, so the emperor ordered Ricci to remain; he was the only one who knew how to start the clocks and keep them going.

After Ricci's death, Johann Adam Schall von Bell took over missionary work in China. By the time of his death in 1666, there were more than 300,000 converts in the kingdom. In 1692, to reward years of Jesuit effort, China passed an edict of toleration. Although it seemed that things were ripe for the conversion of the entire nation, the Jesuits, Dominicans, and Franciscans quarreled over the correct practice of Christianity in China, and things collapsed.

SCHOLASTICISM

The Marriage of Aristotle and Christianity

During the twelfth century there came a revival of learning within the Christian Church. Universities were opening all over Europe, and people began to study, think, and question. Art, literature, music, and science quickly came to the forefront of education.

Cathedral schools were established to promote the understanding of Christianity. These schools were open to all, and their object was to study the faith within the fixed bounds of church law. A cathedral school education consisted of the seven liberal arts:

1. Grammar
2. Rhetoric
3. Logic
4. Arithmetic
5. Geometry
6. Astronomy
7. Music

The growth of education stemmed from enthusiastic schoolteachers, often monastic scholars eager to spread their wealth of knowledge. This enthusiasm would take many educators away from the restrictive bonds of medieval thinking into a mysterious world of questions just dying to be asked.

Gerbert of Rheims

A man named Gerbert of Rheims (later Pope Sylvester II) was a brilliant monastic scholar influenced by both Christian bishops and Muslim culture. Gerbert discovered the inquisitive thinking of Muslim learning and decided to incorporate it into his own teaching methods.

The Value of the Question

One of the most notable intellectuals of the late Middle Ages was Peter Abelard. He gave his inheritance to his brothers and traversed all France to learn from great thinkers. He became a lecturer (professor) at the University of Paris and wrote *Sic et Non* (Latin for *Yes and No*), in which he posted 158 questions with answers drawn from Christian scripture, pagan writings, and church leaders.

Abelard took the ancient Greek method of consistent questioning and applied it to medieval study–something many church leaders did not welcome. At the Council of Soissons in 1121, Abelard was condemned for his writings on the nature of the Trinity and was soon living in seclusion in a monastery. Although his students found him and begged him to continue teaching, Abbot Bernard of Clairvaux, one of the most powerful figures in the church, prevented this and forced Abelard to retire to the abbey of Cluny, where he died in 1142.

Abelard and Héloïse

Abelard was at the center of one of the great sex scandals of the Middle Ages. While teaching in Paris, he became infatuated with Héloïse, niece of the canon of Notre Dame. Abelard seduced her; he made a secret marriage with her, but when Héloïse publicly denied they were married, her uncle confronted Abelard and had him castrated. Héloïse spent the rest of her life in a convent, and the two lovers are today buried together in Paris's Père Lachaise cemetery.

A New Age

Once interest in questioning had begun, there was no way to stop it. Schools opened all over Europe. They developed a teaching method that incorporated Abelard's format of posed questions and answers. The method was called "Scholasticism," which gradually became a means of arriving at difficult conclusions through questions and debate. By arranging information and questioning the details, students would arrive at a logical conclusion.

What's It Mean?

Less than 100 years after Abelard's death, schools opened in Paris, Oxford, Cambridge, and Bologna (among many other cities). The Europeans called these schools *universitas*, which is a Latin word that in the Middle Ages meant any corporate group.

By the end of the thirteenth century, the philosophical writings of the ancient Greeks and other nations outside the empire were flooding over the borders of Europe. Many had been translated from Arabic, since Islamic scholars revered the ancient Greek thinkers and preserved many of their works. The writings of the Jewish philosopher Maimonides and the Muslim thinker Averroes were widely circulated.

St. Thomas Aquinas, a Dominican monk and scholar, was called in to examine the texts of Maimonides and Averroes. While he refuted some of their propositions, he reconciled others with Christian thinking in a massive work titled *Summa Theologica*. The book was never finished, but it is regarded by many scholars as the intellectual high point of the Scholastic movement.

PAUL OF TARSUS

The Man Who Made Christianity

It would be impossible to talk about the growth of Christianity without mentioning the apostle Paul, who was not one of the original apostles. In fact, Paul was an outspoken opponent of Jesus' teachings at first, both during Jesus' life and after his death. It is a surprise then that Paul became a vigilant missionary after he was strangely blinded on the road to Damascus. According to the Bible, the Holy Spirit visited Paul and returned his sight, which then led him as a new convert to spread the message of Jesus and establish Christianity throughout the world—at least the parts of it he could reach in his lifetime.

Paul became the perfect ambassador for Christianity and was able to bridge the gap between Jews, Romans, and Greeks. He had been raised strictly in Judaism; he spoke fluent Greek; and he was a Roman citizen. He was also educated in Greek literature and thought and could, therefore, express the doctrines and teachings of Jesus to the Gentiles. As a Roman citizen, he had certain freedoms that allowed him to travel and continue the work that Jesus began. Paul managed to bring his message to areas of the world that Jesus never reached, such as Turkey and Greece.

Paul's Travels

According to the scriptures, Paul made three major trips during his life:

1. Palestine and Antioch (ancient Syria, now Turkey)
2. Thessalonica (city in ancient Macedonia)
3. Philippi (city in ancient Macedonia) and then on to Corinth and Turkey

However, it wasn't long before authorities caught up to Paul and his continuing Christian teaching. Upon his return to Jerusalem after establishing a church in Ephesus (a city in Turkey), Jewish authorities arrested him, fearing an uprising of Jesus' followers and the possible undermining of Judaism. Paul appealed his case to Rome, where he spent the rest of his life awaiting trial. In A.D. 64, Emperor Nero decided to eradicate the Christians from Rome, and Paul was never seen or heard from again.

New Christian Ground

After the fall of Jerusalem to the Romans in about 70, the seat of the Christian faith had to find new ground. By that time, Christianity had gathered thousands of followers and was powerful enough that finding a new home did not take very long. The second home of the faith was Antioch, where Paul had spent a good deal of time preaching.

Letter to the Thessalonians

On his travels, Paul managed to convert many Gentiles to the teachings of Jesus Christ and during his third trip, he wrote his famous Letter to the Thessalonians, which later became a book in the New Testament.

Christianity found its way into India and northern Africa as Paul made his way to Italy and Spain. By the end of the fourth century—400 years after the birth of Jesus—there were about 500,000 people living in Antioch, and half the population was Christian. By the middle of the third century, there were 30,000 Christians living in Rome.

The New Testament

When Paul got word of newly formed churches that were struggling with certain Christian issues, he wrote many letters to explain the various teachings of Jesus Christ. In an effort to spread the word of God, the Christian leaders often struggled with putting the ideas into effect in a way that everyone could understand. Paul's letters—combined with the writings of the apostles Peter, James, and John, as well as the books written by Mark, Matthew, Luke, and John (the Gospels)—formed the foundation of the new Christian Bible.

CHAPTER 5

ISLAM

The Muslim community is one of the most diverse in the world, ranging from Chinese rice farmers to Bosnian steelworkers; from Indonesian fishermen to Tuareg nomads. Islam spans nearly every continent and plays a key role in the modern political world. Twenty percent of people on Earth consider themselves Muslim.

Despite their differences in language and culture, Muslims share a common faith that brings them a sense of peace and stability in their individual and community lives. Islam guides every aspect of their day-to-day lives, from their choice of work and leisure activities to the food they eat and the way they interact with other people.

Islam has more in common with other religious faiths than many people realize. Muslims believe in One Almighty God and the guidance that He has sent to prophets. Their holy book, the Qur'an, contains stories of such familiar figures as Noah, Moses, Abraham, and Jesus. They honor universal values such as equality, honesty, mercy, and humility.

Yet in today's world, Muslims are often associated with extremism and intolerance; their beliefs are misunderstood and even despised. Stereotypes and misinformation are spread out of ignorance or deliberately promoted for political or social purposes. Isolated cases of violence, many times without any religious motive, stand as examples of what is now considered "normal" Muslim behavior.

When exploring any faith, it's important to look at the totality of its teachings: its basic vocabulary, its holy texts, its prophets, the history of its early faith community, and the interpretations of its modern scholars.

What's It Mean?

The word *Islam*, at its core, means "peaceful worship of and submission to One Almighty God." Those who believe in and practice Islam are known as Muslims, or "those who find peace through trusting submission to and worship of God Alone."

From small and humble beginnings 1,400 years ago, the Muslim community expanded to cover three continents and to lead some of the greatest empires of ancient history. As the foundation for one of the most advanced intellectual and cultural environments of all time, Islam was the embodiment of tolerance, scholarship, and justice. Indeed, it was Muslim leadership that helped to propel Europe out of the Dark Ages and into the modern era. Today, Islam continues to inspire millions of people to lead lives of integrity, innovation, and kindness.

ARTICLES OF FAITH

The Basic Tenets of Islam

Muslims throughout the world share a common set of fundamental beliefs, often described as "articles of faith." These articles of faith form the foundation of the religion of Islam.

Belief in One God

Muslims believe there is only One Supreme God who creates and controls everything in the universe. In Islam, God is believed to be the Creator, the Sustainer, the Ruler, and the Judge. Muslims further recognize that a person who believes in the Creator comes to love Him, trust in Him, hope from Him, and fear disappointing Him.

The Name of God

Allah derives from an Arabic word that means "the God." Arabic-speaking Christians and Jews often use the same name to refer to the Almighty. Muslims see it as the proper name of the One God, as it is the name used in the Qur'an.

Among Muslims, *Allah* is the personal name used for this One Almighty God, a name that is not subject to plurality ("gods") or gender ("goddess"). Sometimes Allah is referred to as "He," or may be quoted in the royal sense, "We." However, in Islam, Allah is beyond all human perception, and is not male, female, dual, or plural. Allah is simply One.

The Attributes of Allah

As God is an unseen being, beyond our limited human perception, it is sometimes difficult for us to imagine His characteristics. The Qur'an offers a description of God by using many different attributes or "names," which help human beings understand the nature of God. The Qur'an says, for example, that He is the Most Merciful, the Most Gracious, the Beneficent, the All-Knowing, the Loving, the All-Wise, and so on.

How Many Attributes or Names?

Traditionally there are ninety-nine different names that are used to describe God in the Qur'an and Sunnah. Muslims often try to recite the names, reflect upon them, and to understand God better through them.

Allah's Relationship with People

While Allah remains beyond all human attempts at understanding, Islam also teaches that Allah fully sustains each and every thing and creature on earth, and He reaches out to us in mercy and compassion. Allah knows everything about every grain of sand, every leaf, and the secret whisperings of each person's heart. One does not need any special devices or intermediaries to reach out directly to Allah.

Muslims believe that Allah created unseen beings, including angels and *jinn*. Angels were created out of light, and they work tirelessly to administer Allah's kingdom. Without a free will of their own, these spiritual creatures carry out Allah's orders in full obedience.

What's It Mean?

The Arabic word for *angels* is *mala'ika*, which comes from the Arabic root meaning "to help and assist," or "gathering, assembly." According to the teachings of Islam, angels give full service and devotion to God, without any hint of disobedience.

The angels surround us at all times, and they have a multitude of duties and tasks. There are angels who record our words and deeds, and those who guard the gates of Heaven and Hell.

The *Jinn*

Unlike the angels, *jinn* are unseen creatures that were created from fire. They have a free will to either obey or disobey Allah, and they will be rewarded or punished on Judgment Day just as human beings will. Muslims believe that *jinn* freely roam the earth and are capable of doing good or harm.

Religion 101 Question

Do Muslims believe in Satan?

Since angels do not have a free will, there is no concept in Islam of a "fallen angel." Muslims believe that Satan (called *Shaytan* or *Iblis* in the Qur'an) is a *jinn* who strives to lead human beings astray.

Belief in the Prophets of God

Muslims believe that it is through Allah's grace and benevolence that He sent prophets and messengers to every nation, in order to guide people to the straight path. Each prophet had different strengths and was born in a different time, place, and culture. However, the prophets' message has always been the same: calling people to worship the One Supreme God and to obey His commandments.

The Qur'an mentions by name nearly thirty different biblical prophets, including Adam, Noah, Abraham, Lot, Jonah, Moses, Aaron, David, Solomon, and Jesus. Muslims honor and revere all of the prophets, understanding that in their own time and place they were exemplary servants of God.

Muhammad, the Last Prophet

As God continued to send prophets to guide His people, they were rejected by their people, and their messages were either distorted or lost. Then Allah would send another prophet to renew and repeat the message of guidance. Muslims believe that after Muhammad, there was no need for Allah to send another prophet, because he left behind the protected scripture of the Qur'an to remain as a guide for mankind.

Muslims believe in the revelation of five divine books:

- *Suhuf* (Scrolls), revealed to Abraham
- *Zabur* (Psalms), revealed to David
- *Tawrah* (Torah), revealed to Moses
- *Injeel* (Gospels), revealed to Jesus
- Qur'an, revealed to Muhammad

Muslims believe these original messages had many teachings in common with Islam at the time they were revealed, although some specific guidance was directed to the communities that received the revelation. Over time, however, the original teachings of these books became distorted or lost, and it was necessary for God to send another message to set the record straight and confirm His teachings. Muslims believe the Qur'an was the final revelation God sent to mankind.

Day of Judgment

Muslims believe that the life of this world and all that is in it will come to an end on one appointed day called *Youm al-Qiyama*, or the Day of Reckoning. At this time, Allah will judge each person individually, according to his or her faith and the balance of his or her good and bad actions.

Belief in Destiny and Divine Decree

The final article of faith is known by many names: *destiny, divine decree, predestination, fate,* or in Arabic, *Al-Qadr.* The Arabic word comes from a root word that means "power" and "ability," implying that God Alone has the power and ability to know the destiny of every creature. Muslims believe that since Allah is the Sustainer of all life, nothing happens except by His Will and with His full knowledge. Everything in the world has a set, predetermined course.

This belief does not contradict the idea that human beings have the free will to choose a course of action. Allah does not force us to do anything; we can choose to obey or disobey Him. However, our choice is known to God before we even do it, because His knowledge is timeless and complete.

PILLARS OF PRACTICE

The Heart of the Muslim World

Muslims observe five formal acts of worship, which they refer to as the five pillars of Islam. Based on the foundation of faith, the pillars of Islam help build and structure a Muslim's daily life. The five pillars of Islam are the declaration of faith, prayer, fasting, almsgiving, and pilgrimage.

Declaration of Faith

To emphasize that Islam is based on a strong monotheistic foundation, the first formal pillar of practice is to declare one's faith in God. A Muslim declares his or her faith by saying, *"La ilaha illa Allah wa Muhammad ar-rasulullah"* ("There is no god worthy to be worshiped except Allah, and Muhammad is the messenger of Allah"). All that is necessary for a person to convert to the faith of Islam is to believe in and make this declaration.

Match Faith with Actions

The declaration of faith is more than just a statement; it must be shown with one's actions.

Daily Prayer

The second pillar of Islam is *salaat* (daily prayer). Muslims perform five formal prayers a day; they rely on these prayers to repeat and refresh their beliefs. The schedule of daily prayer is designed to help Muslims take time out of the busy day to remember Allah and renew the effort to follow His guidance.

Know, therefore, that there is no god but Allah, and ask forgiveness for your faults, and for the men and women who believe. For Allah knows how you move about and how you dwell in your homes.
—Qur'an 47:19

Charitable Giving

In Islam, it is the duty of the wealthy to help those who are poor and destitute.

While charitable giving is always encouraged in Islam, wealthier members of the community are specifically required to pay alms. This practice is known as *zakat*, which comes from an Arabic word for "purify" and "grow," for you purify your own wealth by sharing with others and allowing their wealth to grow.

In addition to *zakat*, voluntary alms (called *sadaqah*) can be given at any time, in any amount, to anyone. The Qur'an repeatedly encourages Muslims to give to the needy and care for orphans.

The Fast of Ramadan

Once each year, Muslims participate in a period of intense spiritual devotion known as the fast of Ramadan. Muslims are commanded to fast during the daylight hours of an entire month.

Liars Beware!

Muhammad once said, "If one does not abandon falsehood in words and deeds, Allah has no need for his abandoning of food and drink." It is therefore imperative that the fasting person not only refrains from food and drink, but also from foul speech, lying, arguing, and the like.

Ramadan allows no food, drink, smoking, or intimacy during the daytime hours of the month. From dawn until dusk, Muslims must practice self-control and focus on prayers and devotion. During the fast, Muslims experience hunger and thirst and learn to sympathize with those in the world who have little to eat. They come to appreciate the blessings that Allah grants them.

On a day of fasting, Muslims rise before dawn for an early meal called *suhoor*. This light meal is intended to nourish the body through the rigorous daylong fast. The fast begins with the predawn call to prayer. Muslims continue through their daily lives of work, school, or other commitments, conscious of the limitations of fasting, and striving to be on their best behavior. Muslims continue to observe the daily prayers as usual and often spend part of the day reading chapters of the Qur'an.

As sunset approaches, Muslims often gather together as family or community to break the fast and enjoy a meal together at the end of the day. Muslims break their fast just as the call for the sunset prayer is heard.

Hajj: The Pilgrimage to Mecca

Every Muslim strives to make a once-in-a-lifetime pilgrimage to the sacred sites in Mecca, in present-day Saudi Arabia. This final pillar of Islam is required of every adult Muslim, male or female, if it is physically and financially possible. Many Muslims spend their entire lives saving and planning for this journey.

When undertaking the pilgrimage, Muslims first shed all signs of their wealth and status by donning simple white garments, called *ihram*, a symbol of purity and equality. When wearing the *ihram*, the pilgrims enter a state of devotion and purity.

1. On the first day of the Hajj, the pilgrims travel from Mecca to Mina, a small village east of the city. There they spend the day and night, praying and reading the Qur'an.

2. On the second day of the pilgrimage, the pilgrims leave Mina just after dawn to travel to the plain of Arafat for the culminating experience of the Hajj. On what is known as the "Day of Arafat," the pilgrims spend the entire day standing near the Mount of Mercy, asking Allah for forgiveness and making supplications. After sunset, the pilgrims leave and travel to an open plain called Muzdalifah. There they spend the night praying, and they collect small stone pebbles to be used on the next day.

3. On the third day, the pilgrims move before sunrise, this time back to Mina. Here they throw the stone pebbles at pillars that represent the seductions of Satan. After casting the pebbles, most pilgrims slaughter an animal (often a sheep or a goat) and give the meat to the poor—a symbolic act that shows their willingness to part with something that is precious to them, just as the Prophet Abraham was prepared to sacrifice his son at God's command.

4. The pilgrims then return to Mecca and perform seven turns around the *Ka'aba*, the house of worship built by Abraham and his son Ishmael. In other rites, the pilgrims pray near a place called "the Station of Abraham," which is reportedly where Abraham stood while constructing the Ka'aba. The pilgrims also walk seven times between two small hills near the Ka'aba, called Safa and Marwa, in remembrance of the plight of Abraham's wife

Hajar, who searched desperately for water for herself and her son before a spring welled up in the desert for her. The pilgrims also drink from this ancient spring, which continues to flow today.

Why Are Only Muslims Allowed into Mecca and Madinah?

These are cities of great importance in Islamic tradition, centers of pilgrimage and prayer, sacred places where Muslims are free from the distractions of daily life. The ban, mentioned in the Qur'an, is intended to provide a place of peace and refuge for Muslim believers.

The Lesser Pilgrimage or Umrah

Hajj is required of every adult Muslim who is physically and financially able to make the journey, and it must be performed during a specific period of time in the Islamic calendar. However, there is another type of pilgrimage to Mecca, known as the *umrah* (lesser pilgrimage), which may be performed any time during the year.

JIHAD: THE HOLY STRUGGLE

The True Meaning of a Misunderstood Word

Perhaps one of the most controversial and misunderstood aspects of Islam is the concept of jihad. Some groups of Muslims misinterpret the idea of jihad, limiting its sense to an armed struggle against outsiders. However, the original Islamic meaning of this term referred to a complex internal and external struggle to practice faith in the midst of oppression.

What's It Mean?

The word *jihad* comes from the Arabic root *J-H-D*, which carries the meaning "struggle" or "strive." Other words derived from this root include "effort," "fatigue," and "labor." The essential meaning is this: Jihad is a struggle to practice one's faith in the face of obstacles. The translation of *jihad* as "holy war" is incorrect. In Arabic, you would translate "holy war" as *harbun muqaddasatu*, a phrase that is not found in the Qur'an or in any other form of Islamic literature.

The word *jihad* appears in the Qur'an several times, where it is used to describe the efforts of the believers to resist pressure from others to give up their faith and to defend themselves against oppressors.

Jihad in Practice

During the lifetime of the Prophet Muhammad, the Muslim community was in a struggle for its very survival. Faced with the persecution and cruelty of the people of Mecca, the Muslims sought alternative means of defense. They immigrated to Abyssinia and then to Madinah, enforced economic blockades, and formed peace treaties and alliances.

There were times when the Muslims engaged in battle. In these cases, verses of the Qur'an were revealed, advising them to fight strong and hard. Without exception, the early Muslims fought in battles only to defend themselves against unprovoked attack or the betrayal of false allies.

The Qur'an repeatedly stresses the value of forgiveness, even toward one's enemies. While Islam generally holds to the ancient teaching of "an eye for an eye," there is an emphasis on the blessings of forgiveness.

No Forced Conversions

Although in Islam *jihad* refers first to the spiritual struggle of a believer rather than the physical, violent struggles of war, jihad today is most often understood only as the latter. According to Islamic doctrine, however, if faith does not emerge from deep personal conviction, it is neither truthful nor acceptable to God. Faith is a matter of the heart, between one's self and God.

The Qur'an often describes defensive jihad as a system of checks and balances, a way that Allah set up to "check one set of people by means of another" (Qur'an 2:251 and other verses). Muslims are called upon to respond to aggression and persecution, and take it as their duty to stop anyone who transgresses justice.

Even during the times when Muslims are engaged in battles of a military nature, they must follow certain codes of ethics and rules of engagement laid down in the Qur'an and exemplified by the life of the Prophet Muhammad. It is human nature to become agitated and seek revenge when one is wronged, so Islam lays out very strict rules to ensure the legitimate and proper conduct of Muslim soldiers.

Some of the rules include the following:

- Give diplomacy a chance before battle starts; respect all treaties.
- Do not harm those who are not physically involved in fighting.
- Do not destroy property, including real estate, infrastructure, trees, farms, animals, and orchards.
- Protect all places of worship.
- Treat well all prisoners of war.
- Allow the bodies of soldiers slain in battle to be buried in dignity.
- Stop fighting when the enemy ceases hostilities and negotiate for peace.

It is particularly sinful to deliberately kill one's self. Suicide is usually an act of desperation by a person who has no sense of the value of his or her own life. Allah advises Muslims to be patient, hopeful, and confident of the mercy of Allah, and not to despair or lose hope.

Consequences of Suicide

According to Islamic tradition, people who commit suicide will spend their time in Hell torturing themselves with their chosen method or weapon. A person who jumps off a cliff, for example, will spend eternity jumping off cliffs and feeling the agony of death over and over again.

Islam teaches that sacrifice, bravery, and sincere effort will be rewarded by Allah in the Hereafter. The Arabic word for martyr is *shaheed*, which means "witness." A true martyr witnesses the truth and gives up his or her life for it, dying under brave or heroic circumstances.

Muhammad once said that there are people who kill in the name of Islam but still go to Hellfire. When asked why, he answered, "Because they were not truly fighting for the sake of God." To be considered a martyr, one must be acting within the bounds of Islamic law and have pure intentions.

The Middle Path

The words *fundamentalist* and *extremist* are often used interchangeably in today's world. Muslims prefer to draw a distinction between those who follow the basic principles (fundamentals) of their faith and those who join the extreme, fanatic fringe.

In the Qur'an, Muslims are instructed to be moderate in all affairs of life, especially on issues concerning religion.

Muhammad advised his followers to practice kindness and bring people together. In one tradition, he told the people to "make things easy and convenient, and do not make them hard or difficult. Give cheers and glad tidings, and do not create tension or hatred, nor repel others."

Returning to the Fundamentals

In Islam, being a fundamentalist does not mean that one is an extremist. For Muslims, fundamentalism means strictly following one's religious text. In this sense, all Muslims are fundamentalist by nature because they strive to adhere to the basic principles of their faith as described in the Qur'an. There are many Muslims today who follow the fundamental teachings of Islam but are unfairly labeled as radical extremists.

No Room for Terrorism

The Qur'an clearly condemns actions that transgress beyond what is considered lawful and just. Acts of terrorism, including the murder of innocent civilians, are certainly considered transgressions beyond the limits of justice.

Throughout Islamic history, acts of transgression were dealt with harshly to deter anyone else from believing that such actions have merit or are useful ways to further a cause. Islamic courts have upheld capital punishment for those convicted of piracy, airplane hijacking, kidnapping, and genocide. Muslim leaders and individuals all over the world express condemnation and outrage when acts of terrorism are perpetrated upon innocent people, whether the terrorists are so-called Muslims or not.

ISLAMIC INTELLECTUAL TRADITIONS

The House of Wisdom

At the height of the Islamic empire, the Muslim world was the center for learning. Scholars of many faiths traveled from all over the world to participate in research and scholarly exchanges in the large Muslim cities. Indeed, several centers of learning gathered students, teachers, and researchers to live and study together. They were the first organized schools in the Muslim world.

In the early years of Islam, those with religious knowledge informally tutored a group of students. Over time, more formal institutions of education were founded. The *madrasahs*, or schools for the training of religious and societal leaders, still exist today.

The Importance of Literacy

Islam places a very high value on literacy. Even during the early years, when Muslims were engaged in wars of defense, enemy prisoners of war could earn their freedom by teaching ten young Muslims how to read and write. Both girls and boys are encouraged to attend school, and in many Muslim countries, women outnumber men in university programs.

There were several fundamental principles of the *madrasah*. First was the idea that all knowledge must be based on a strong spiritual foundation. Second, education was to be open to all, including both boys and girls, on equal terms. Finally, while religious studies served as a foundation, the curriculum also included many other disciplines, including literature and poetry, mathematics and astronomy, and chemistry and the natural sciences.

For adult education, one of the most remarkable assemblies of scholars took place in Baghdad at the Bayt al-Hikmah (House of Wisdom). It was organized by Caliph al-Mamun, the son of Harun al-Rashid. In the eighth century, al-Mamun received permission from the Byzantine emperor to access the libraries of Constantinople and other cities. Scholars were dispatched to collect the scientific and philosophical manuscripts of the ancient Greeks, which were brought back to Baghdad for translation and study.

Religion 101 Question

What is the oldest university in the world?

The Quaraouiyine (Karaouine) University in Fez, Morocco, has the distinction of being the oldest continuously operating university in the world. This center of learning was founded by a Muslim woman, Fatima El-Fihria, in 859. The second-oldest university in the world (Al-Azhar) was founded in Egypt in the tenth century.

At Bayt al-Hikmah, scholars from around the world gathered to translate the Greek manuscripts and conduct their own independent research in the free academic environment. These scholars made incredible achievements in mathematics, geometry, astronomy, and medicine.

Famous Muslim Scientists

The Muslim world did more than just translate ancient works and pass them on to Europe at the end of the Dark Ages. Over the centuries, these works were studied, incorporated into the current framework of knowledge, and then expounded. Among the most notable achievements of Arab scholars were the introduction of Arabic numerals, the study of algebra, medical anatomical drawings, advances in optics, geographical maps, and the production of several scientific instruments, such as the astrolabe (used in ancient times to determine the position of the sun and stars).

Islamic scholars took up the study of Greek medicine very early on. Translators at Bayt al-Hikmah worked diligently to translate the works of Hippocrates, Dioscorides, Galen, and others into Arabic. Harun al-Rashid created the first modern hospital in Baghdad in 805.

Abu Bakr Al-Razi is one of the best-known contributors to medical knowledge. A native of Persia (present-day Iran, near Tehran), Al-Razi traveled to Baghdad to study medicine and later became director of a large hospital there. He wrote more than 200 books and was a master of observation and experimental medicine. Another great Muslim medical scholar is known in the West as Avicenna. Abu Ali ibn Sina was born in tenth-century Bukhara, Persia (present-day Uzbekistan). Ibn Sina was a young prodigy, engaging in studies of medicine, philosophy, and poetry.

Astronomy

The study of astronomy developed in Islamic society because of a religious need. Scholars needed to observe and study the sun and moon in order to determine the months of the lunar calendar, figure out the prayer and fasting times, and find the direction of the *qiblah* (direction of Mecca for prayer). Islamic scholars mapped the celestial sky, figured celestial orbits, and questioned the accuracy of Ptolemy's theories.

How High Is the Sky?

The Muslim physicist Ibn Al-Haytham (965–1040) calculated the height of Earth's atmosphere at 52,000 paces, which is equivalent to about thirty-two miles. His calculations were very accurate for the time; modern scholarship has concluded that the atmosphere extends thirty-one miles from Earth.

Muslim scientists built observatories all over the Islamic world and refined and revised Ptolemy's catalog and coordinates for the stars. They also excelled in making astronomical instruments. In the eleventh century, Nasir Al-Tusi (1201–1274) of Baghdad invented the azimuth quadrant and the torquetum, early instruments used to compute and measure star positions.

One of the greatest mathematicians who ever lived was Abu Abdullah al-Khawarizmi (c. 780–c. 850). Born in modern-day Uzbekistan, he was raised near Baghdad and was associated with the great institutions of learning there. Al-Khawarizmi is known as the founder of algebra, and he also introduced the concept of the algorithm. Al-Khawarizmi also developed solutions for linear and quadratic equations and detailed trigonometric tables and geometric and arithmetical concepts.

Another famous mathematician, Abu Raihan Al-Biruni (973–1048), wrote about Earth's rotation, made calculations of latitude and longitude, and used mathematical techniques to determine the seasons. As well he discussed the speed of light versus the speed of sound and accurately determined the weights of more than a dozen elements and compounds.

Geography

Many Muslim scientists were involved in the development of geographical knowledge. Muslims were among the first to calculate Earth's circumference, publish detailed world maps, and study elements and minerals. Muslim geographers traveled all over the world to gather data.

Under the leadership of the mathematician Al-Khawarizmi, seventy geographers worked together to produce the first map of the globe, in 830. One of the better-known geographers was Al-Idrisi (1099–c. 1166), who was hired to produce a world map for the Norman King of Sicily, Roger II. Several of Al-Idrisi's books were translated into Latin, and his work spread rapidly through Europe. Christopher Columbus used a map that was derived from Al-Idrisi's work in his explorations of the New World.

English Words of Arabic Origin

The Muslim world had an incredible influence on the discovery and development of modern scientific ideas. This influence is reflected in the many English words that originated from the Arabic language.

WORDS OF ARABIC ORIGIN	
English	**Arabic**
admiral	*amir*
alchemy	*al-kimiya*
alcohol	*al-kohl*
alcove	*al-qubba*
algebra	*al-Jabr*
algorithm	*al-Khawarizmi*
almanac	*al-manaakh*
atlas	*atlas*
camphor	*kafur*
cipher/zero	*sifr*
cornea	*al-qarniya*
cotton	*al-qutn*
elixir	*al-aksir*
gauze	*al-gazz*
monsoon	*mawsim*
safari	*safara*
sofa	*suffa*
talc	*talq*
typhoon	*tufaan*
vizier	*waxir*
zenith	*semit*

THE QUR'AN

Sacred Teachings of Muhammad

Millions of people take the Qur'an as a guidebook to life. The ancient text discusses hundreds of topics on all aspects of life, including science, ethics, justice, history, social order, faith, and the afterlife. Along with the teachings of Prophet Muhammad, the Qur'an provides everything a Muslim needs to know about Islamic faith.

Facts about the Qur'an

- The text was revealed about 1,400 years ago to Prophet Muhammad.
- The original language of the Qur'an is Arabic.
- It is the last of all Holy Books.
- Revelation of the Qur'an did not happen all at once, but occurred over the course of about twenty-three years.

The Qur'an is made up of 114 Surahs (or Suras)—the Arabic term for a Qur'anic chapter—of varying lengths. A Surah is composed of numbered verses, with the longest Surah containing 286 verses. The Surahs were revealed in parts to the Prophet on certain occasions, and not in the order they are placed in the Qur'an. Qur'anic verses are referenced by Surah and verse; for example 33:36 means Surah 33, verse 36.

A Way of Life

Islam emerged from the Qur'an: without it there would be no Islam. It provides everything Muslims need to know about their religion. Although the Qur'an is fairly straightforward and logical, because of its extensiveness, it can seem inaccessible for people who don't understand it well.

The Qur'an talks about an abundance of subjects. Apart from awing readers with its beautiful prose, it also awes scientists with surprisingly accurate information about microbiology, physiology, astronomy, and many other fields. Additionally, it is a book of historic recollections, telling stories about the prophets that came before Muhammad, such as Solomon, Abraham, and Moses.

Another important aspect of the Qur'an is that much of its text preaches high moral standards, urging people to abide by a strict code of ethics. For example, the Qur'an strongly condemns hypocrisy, fraud, and gossip, and encourages good qualities such as modesty, truthfulness, and kindness.

Above all, though, the Qur'an's most significant objective is to allow humankind to learn about the Creator. As Allah speaks to humankind through the Qur'an, He tells them that He is the sole Supreme Being and the one and only Creator. He has no partners or family. He has full control of the universe and all that He created, and He is the only one to be worshiped.

In the Original

You can find the Qur'an sold in every corner of the globe, translated into most of the world's languages. However, Muslims stress the importance of reading the Qur'an in its original language, Arabic, believing that translations dilute the message and take away from its natural beauty.

The Relationship Between Qur'an and Sunnah

As Islam is derived from the Qur'an, the smaller details are derived from the teachings of the Prophet. These teachings are called *Sunnah*.

Some Sunnah have to do with the way the Prophet carried out his daily life. Others give the Prophet's explanation of Qur'anic text. These clarifications are found in the Hadith—quotes and anecdotes of Muhammad. There are thousands of Hadith that Muslims use to understand the Qur'an and Allah's instructions thoroughly. A simple example would be as follows: The Qur'an states in reference to ablution, or ritual cleansing, that a person must wash his arms to the elbows, and his face, head, and feet. Prophet Muhammad complements the Qur'an by teaching his followers exactly how to wash, what other body parts to include, and the number of repetitions.

From a general perspective, the Qur'an and the Sunnah are the two sources of Islam. The Qur'an comes first, then the Sunnah complements it, explaining and clarifying what is difficult for the people to understand. Prophet Muhammad provided guidance through his Hadith and gave the people an example to follow. Muslims consider him the role model for Islam, and his teachings cannot be separated from the teachings of the Qur'an.

Ablution

According to Islamic teachings, ablution is a standard requirement before most acts of worship. The Qur'an and Sunnah teach that the hands, mouth, nostrils, arms, face, head, ears, and feet must be washed or wiped with clean water in that particular order to qualify as proper ablution.

When scholars debate over a certain Islamic topic, they use quotes from the Qur'an and Sunnah to support their arguments. If a supporting statement they want is not available in the Qur'an, they quote a Hadith. The Hadith are integral to the survival of Islam. There are a few thousand of them that are available to answer common questions and interpret many verses in the Qur'an. They address specific Islamic situations or problems and propose solutions.

A Hadith is almost always a quote of Prophet Muhammad from someone who was present with the Prophet at the moment he said it. Usually, a Hadith is preceded by the name of the person who transmitted the information, such as, "According to Aisha, Prophet Muhammad said so and so."

The Hadith is the word of Muhammad, not Allah. The Hadith were not preserved as well as the Qur'an, and scholars say that a few Hadith underwent slight distortion as they were transmitted from reference to reference. Therefore, Hadith have three classifications: authenticated Hadith, valid Hadith, and weak Hadith. An authenticated Hadith is a real and accurate quote of Muhammad. A valid Hadith is less established and its integrity suffers from a minor degree of doubt. A weak Hadith is just what the name implies—the Prophet may or may not have said it.

Qudsi Hadith

A Qudsi Hadith, also known as Hadith Qudsi (holy), is Allah's words narrated through the Prophet; for example, Prophet Muhammad said, "On Judgment Day, Allah will speak to the people of heaven, telling them . . ." A Qudsi Hadith quotes Allah Himself, but in a manner and style different from the Qur'an.

The Qur'an and the Sunnah set rules Muslims must follow when attempting to read the Qur'an. Before even touching the Holy Book, the body must be cleansed through ablution. Allah specifies this in the Qur'an: "That (this) is indeed a noble Qur'an. In a book kept hidden. Which none touches but the purified. A revelation from the Lord of the Worlds" (56:77–80).

Reading the Qur'an

When reading the Qur'an it is important to take a reasonably respectful posture. According to Islam, sitting at your desk, in an armchair, or on a ground cushion with your legs crossed are all acceptable positions, but leaning back in your seat and throwing your legs over your desk is not!

Muslims regularly pick up and read the Qur'an, even if they have already read it many times before. No matter how many times it is read, there is always a new discovery or enlightenment, or a lesson learned. Muslims take it as a guide for life that takes the effort out of deciding where one belongs, and why one exists. They believe it sets down a path to be followed.

ISLAMIC LAW AND CUSTOMS

Faith and Charity

The Islamic Shari'ah is the entire legal system implemented in Islam. The word itself implies an endless source of water from which people satisfy their thirst.

The Islamic penal code provides for harsh punishments (for example, the penalty for theft is cutting off of one hand). Punishments such as these are meted out only for crimes that are considered transgressions against the community, because they put the entire society at risk. Only an Islamic court of law may order these sentences, and in reality, they are rarely carried out.

Major and Minor Sins

Islam classifies sins according to the severity of their consequences on individuals and society, with the harshest of warnings reserved for those actions that have the potential of harming the community as a whole.

A major sin in Islam is one that is directly warned against in the Qur'an. Among the major sins are such acts as murder, theft, perjury, bribery, slander, adultery, drinking alcohol, and fighting unjustly between people. They also include violations against God, such as polytheism or neglect of religious duties.

One may also make minor violations; these have not been given a specific punishment in the Qur'an. Examples of minor sins in Islam include bragging, flirting, lying, and swearing.

Repentance

In Islam, almost all sins can be forgiven by God if one truly repents and vows not to repeat the same mistake. Repentance is known as *tauba* in Arabic, which means "to turn back." In order to repent, one must recognize the sin and give it up, and one must feel a sense of remorse for the act. Then one resolves never to make the same mistake again. If the action has caused harm to any other person, one must attempt to make amends by compensating them (if possible) or seeking their forgiveness.

Religion 101 Question

Must a Muslim confess a sin to someone?

No. In Islam, repentance is directly between an individual and God, without any intermediaries.

Dietary Laws

The Qur'an specifies certain foods that Muslims are prohibited from eating, including the following:

- Swine, including all pork byproducts
- Animals slaughtered in dedication to false gods
- Blood or dead carcasses
- Animals that have been strangled, beaten to death, gored, eaten by wild animals, or that have died as the result of a fall
- Predatory animals (carnivores such as lions, dogs, eagles, owls, and others)

Food of the Book

In recognition of their similarities in faith, the Qur'an permits Muslims to eat food provided by the "People of the Book" (Jews, Christians, or other monotheists), as long as the other Islamic dietary rules are also followed.

When slaughtering animals for food, Muslims recognize they are taking life that God has made sacred. They thus invoke God's name as a reminder that they are killing with His permission, only to meet the need for food.

There is a zero-tolerance policy in Islam toward alcohol and drugs. Nowadays, many medical doctors propose that there are benefits to moderate consumption of some substances, such as wine and marijuana. However, Islam takes the strong prohibitive stance.

Many Muslims believe that tobacco and nicotine are poisons to the body and are therefore to be avoided. The strong link between smoking and serious health problems, such as cancer and heart disease, is the main reason cited for its prohibition.

Financial Prohibitions

In Islam, people are encouraged to earn a living and support their families. Exploitation and corruption cause harm to individuals and the community, and they weaken an economy based on honest, hard work.

In the Qur'an, gambling is discussed in the same verses as alcohol. Both are described as having some "profit for men," but "the sin is greater than the profit" (Qur'an 2:219). The Qur'an refers to gambling as a "game of chance," and scholars have interpreted that to include lotteries, casino gambling, or even betting on the outcomes of races or sports events.

Islam absolutely prohibits the lending of money for a price or with a fixed rate of interest. Interest-based lending creates an atmosphere where the wealthy exploit the weak, creating greed and hatred in people's hearts. This guideline, like all of the others in Islam, is in place to help people engage in fair, trusting relationships with each other, and to help them avoid potential exploitation and abuse.

Men and Women

Islam teaches men and women to coexist in cooperation, without exceeding the limits defined for them in Islam. When Muslim men and women are in the presence of each other, they must observe guidelines that help them retain an air of respect, politeness, and honor. Islam forbids any situation that may lead to improper, unlawful, or suspicious circumstances.

In the Qur'an, both men and women are commanded to be modest and "lower their eyes." This means that they should be humble and not gaze at each other in an immodest way.

Islam prohibits all forms of public nudity and exploitation of the female body. Muslim women are advised in the Qur'an not to make a display of their beauty in public.

In ancient times, it was customary for women to wear a head covering often called a *hijab* or *khimar*. Women are advised to wear garments over their house clothes when they leave the house. This outer garment is often called a *jilbab*, *abaya*, or *chador*, depending on the area of the world.

The Qur'an makes no reference to color or style, so one will find many local variations that meet these basic standards. On the Arabian Peninsula, it is customary for women to wear black. In western Africa, women wear colorful dresses and turbans. In Southeast Asia, women often wear *shalwar kameez*, tunics and pants of bright colors and designs. Islam allows for local variations as an expression of the diversity of the Muslim community, as long as minimum standards are observed.

In the privacy of the home, or in the presence only of family members and close female friends, Muslim women are free to remove their head coverings and outer garments and adorn themselves with makeup and jewelry.

In the vast majority of Muslim nations, women are free to choose their style of dress and whether they would like to "cover" or not. It is a personal choice based on piety and modesty and is not considered a sign of women's inferiority by those who practice it.

Islam also prohibits all forms of nudity and exploitation of the male figure. Men are advised to cover their bodies modestly, particularly from the navel to the knee. Indeed, in the traditional dress of many Muslim countries, men wear long flowing robes and sometimes a head covering as well.

Fair Business Practices

In Islam, it is expected that any earnings will be made through decent and honest labor. Business practices must be conducted with frankness and honesty. Islam encourages that contracts and agreements should be written down and witnessed by two trustworthy persons so neither party can try to take advantage of the other or make false claims in the future.

Prompt Payment

Muslims are encouraged to pay for services as soon as they are performed and not to withhold or delay payment. Muhammad instructed that when Muslims hire laborers to do some work, they should "compensate them before the sweat dries."

DIVISIONS WITHIN ISLAM

Sunni and Shi'ite

The very first division in Islam, between Sunni and Shi'a, occurred not as a matter of differing beliefs, but due to politics and the role of leadership in the community. The issue centered on the question of who was to lead the Muslim community following Muhammad's death.

When Muhammad was suffering from his final illness, he appointed his closest companion, Abu Bakr (573–634), to lead the community in prayer. After Muhammad's death, many of his companions felt that leadership of the community should go to the person most suited to the task. They consulted among themselves and selected Abu Bakr, in line with Islamic teachings about consultation and agreement among elders. Those who agreed with Abu Bakr's appointment became known as Sunni (followers of the tradition of Muhammad).

Other members of the community felt that leadership of the Muslim state should stay within the bloodline of Muhammad, within his own family. Particularly, they felt that Muhammad's son-in-law, Ali, should have been appointed the next leader of the community. This group became known as Shi'ati Ali (supporters of Ali). Due to political loyalties and deepening mutual distrust, Shi'a Muslims rejected or altered some practices of Islam.

Sunni Muslims shun formal clergy status, recognizing only jurists and scholars who offer nonbinding opinions. In contract, Shi'a Muslim leaders have popelike authority.

Shi'a Muslims tend to focus more on the virtues of martyrdom.

Today, Shi'a Muslims make up approximately 10 percent of the world's Muslims. They are found mostly in Iran, with large communities in Kuwait, Lebanon, Iraq, and Bahrain. Their tensions have been an important factor in events such as the Iraq War.

A Mystical Faith: Sufism

In the early centuries after Muhammad's death, some Muslims became disenchanted with the Islamic community's growing interest in worldly affairs and the rigid application of rules within the faith. These self-described purists dedicated themselves to frugal living and getting in the spirit of faith. They strove to purify the soul and develop a connection with Allah. The path of the Sufis is often called the mystic or spiritual trend within Islam.

What's It Mean?

The word *sufi* comes from the Arabic word for wool (*suf*). Followers of this trend traditionally wore wool because of its simplicity and low cost. *Sufi* may also be related to the word "to clean" (*safa*), since the Sufis were interested in cleansing the soul.

Over time Sufis organized various orders, each of which is called a *tariqa* (path). A Sufi master, called a *shaykh*, serves as the leader and guide to his followers. Sufis develop an intense devotion to their shaykh because they believe he can provide spiritual guidance and healing for those under his care.

The Qadiani Movement

The Qadiani, or Ahmadiyya, movement began in the late nineteenth century in the Punjab region of India, where a Muslim reformer named Mirza Ghulam Ahmad first claimed that he was the promised Messiah and later that he was a prophet of Allah who received divine revelation.

The followers of Ahmed have established what is known as the Ahmadiyya Mission to propagate their teachings and invite others to follow their path. They are known for preparing and distributing multilingual translations of the Qur'an but with variations in the text that support their own interpretations of Islamic teachings and history.

Muslims consider Ghulam Ahmad a false prophet, and all Muslim scholars consider Qadianis to be outside the fold of Islam.

Sects Within Sects

The Ahmadiyya are also called Qadiani because their founder was from the city of Qadian in the Punjab province of India. There is a further break within the group among those who persist in the belief that Ahmad was a prophet, and those who respect him as a spiritual leader but fall short of calling him a prophet.

The Khalifites

This relatively new group believes that the Qur'an is the only source of guidance in Islam, and that the traditions of Muhammad and the other prophets are irrelevant. They reject the entire Sunnah (words and acts of Muhammad), and depend solely on the Qur'an.

The Khalifites claim that there is an intricate mathematical code in the Qur'an, proving that it is indeed the word of God and could not possibly have been written by any man. This mathematical "miracle" is based on the number nineteen. Letters and verses are counted, given numerological values, added and multiplied, and statistically determined to be equivalent to the number nineteen or a multiple of nineteen.

For some time, scholars were intrigued by this claim and investigated it. Over time, however, the methodology used by the Khalifites came under question. It was discovered that they had revised the Qur'an so that words and verses would fit into their formula. The statistics were determined to be false, and the theory, questionable at first, was later determined to be fraudulent.

The Baha'i Faith

The Baha'i faith arose from Islam and has now grown to be a worldwide religion. The Baha'i believe in the unity of God and in the essential message that has been revealed through the prophets over time. They recognize Muhammad as a prophet but also believe that Krishna, Buddha, and others were "Great Manifestations of God," culminating in the teachings of the founder of their faith, Bahaullah.

In Muslim Persia during the nineteenth century, a young man called the Bab (the Gate) announced the imminent arrival of a messenger of God. Although he was executed as a heretic in 1850, thirteen years later, in 1863, a man named Bahaullah (meaning "the Glory of God" in Arabic) announced that he was the fulfillment of the Bab's promise. He was first imprisoned, then exiled. From exile he wrote a series of letters and documents outlining his views of universal peace and a united world civilization. He died in 1892, but his writings and teachings, at first obscure, have become the basis for a faith that has sustained millions of Baha'i around the world.

World Peace

The Baha'i believe in the unity of the world's great religions, that they all came from the same spiritual source. The central theme of their faith is that humans form one single race and are destined to be unified in one world society. Followers of this faith are heavily involved in issues of world peace, world government, freedom, and equality.

MUHAMMAD

The Last Prophet

Muhammad the Prophet is a central figure in the faith of Islam. Raised as an orphan, he grew up to become a respected merchant. He was a spiritual and reflective man who led a faith community that impacted the entire world. Muslims honor and respect the Prophet Muhammad, and look to his life example for inspiration and guidance.

The Path of the Prophets

Muslim tradition holds that there have been more than 124,000 prophets sent to mankind throughout history, beginning with Adam and ending with Muhammad. Only twenty-five are mentioned by name in the Qur'an, and Muslims do not speculate about the identities of others.

Early Life in Mecca

Muhammad was born around 569–570 in Mecca, modern-day Saudi Arabia, into a respected tribe, the Quraish. Orphaned at six years of age, he was cared for by members of his extended family.

As Muhammad grew older, he became known in the community as a person of integrity and honesty. He married a wealthy businesswoman in Mecca, named Khadijah, fifteen years his senior. The couple would remain happily married until Khadijah's death twenty-five years later. Muhammad and Khadijah had two sons, both of whom died in infancy, and four daughters: Zainab, Ruqaiyah, Um Kulthum, and Fatima.

During the month of Ramadan, Muhammad frequently visited nearby mountains to spend time in quiet solitude and prayer. He would often retire to a particular cave named Hira, located in the hills not far from Mecca, for worship and contemplation. During one of these retreats in the year 610, at the age of forty, Muhammad had an extraordinary experience.

One night toward the end of the month of Ramadan, the angel Gabriel appeared to Muhammad and demanded, "Read!" Muhammad reportedly answered, "I cannot read," for he was illiterate. The angel repeated the request several times and then relayed the beginnings of a revelation from God.

Following this incredible experience, Muhammad rushed home and told Khadijah what had happened. She covered him with blankets, consoled him, and reminded him that he had always been a man of charity and honesty, and that God would not lead him astray.

Preaching the Message of God

When Muhammad began to preach his mission, he first spoke secretly with members of his own family. Then he shared the message with his closest friends and members of his own tribe. Several years after first receiving revelation, he finally reached the point at which he was proclaiming God's message publicly in the city.

After this first encounter, Muhammad experienced a brief pause in revelation. During this time of waiting, he devoted himself more to prayers and spiritual devotion. Then the revelations continued, with the command to "arise and warn" (Qur'an 74:2), "rehearse and proclaim . . . the bounty of God" (Qur'an 93:11), and to "admonish your nearest kinsmen" (Qur'an 26:214).

Preaching and Persecution

The leaders of Mecca were not pleased with Muhammad's message. He was commanding the people to reject the tribal idols that were the financial mainstay of the city. He encouraged people to be charitable and to free their slaves. He condemned the traditionally held beliefs and practices of the most powerful tribes in the city. He preached the Oneness of God in Mecca, the main center of idolatry.

After months of worsening abuse and murders at the hands of their opponents, the Muslims began to look outside Mecca for refuge. In the fifth year of his mission, Muhammad sent a small group of followers to the safety of Abyssinia.

Those Muslims who did not emigrate faced the increased wrath of the Meccan opposition. At the same time Muhammad suffered two deep personal losses. His protective uncle, Abu Talib, and his devoted wife, Khadijah, both passed away in what became known as the "year of sadness." However, it was during this time, when Muhammad's mission seemed to be at its weakest, that he was granted a beautiful sign from God.

Muslim tradition holds that during one night, Muhammad traveled to the far holy city of Jerusalem and from there ascended up to the heavens. During the ascension, Muhammad was welcomed by the previous prophets and was commanded by God to implement the five daily prayers.

The Migration (Hijrah)

Meanwhile, the hostility of the pagan Meccans increased. Muhammad finally found a group of sympathetic people from the city of Yathrib, about 275 miles north of Mecca. They invited Muhammad and his followers to migrate to their city, where the Muslims would be sheltered, protected, and treated as family.

In 622, the entire Muslim community finally succeeded in reaching Yathrib safely. The migration itself is called the *hijrah*, or migration. From that point on, the city of Yathrib became known as Madinah An-Nabi ("The City of the Prophet") or Madinah Al-Munawwarah ("The Radiant City").

In Madinah, the new community set about the business of living, farming, and freely practicing their faith. For the first time, the Muslims could organize society the way they believed it should be, in accordance with the guidance that Muhammad continued to receive from God. The community built a mosque for prayer, established societal rules, and set aside old tribal struggles and blood feuds.

Shortly after arriving in Madinah, Muhammad invited representatives from neighboring tribes—Jews, Christians, and others—to discuss the idea of establishing a city-state in Madinah. With their approval, Muhammad established the first written constitution, which defined his role as leader of the community and the rights and duties of all citizens.

Muhammad traveled to other cities and tribes in the area to engage them in treaties of alliance. At the same time, the Meccans continued to threaten and harass them, so the Muslims fortified themselves against possible attack. Following the battles of Badr and Uhud, Muhammad was able to strengthen the alliances he had forged with various tribes.

Conquest of Mecca

Eventually, Muhammad negotiated a return to Mecca, including terms for a ten-year ceasefire, and agreed to remain neutral in conflicts with third parties. The armistice would allow both sides to live in happiness and to conduct their own affairs freely.

Not very long after signing the treaty, a tribe that had allied with the Meccans attacked a tribe that had allied with the Muslims. Muhammad responded by leading an army of 10,000 into Mecca. The Meccans were so surprised by the size of the Muslim army that they surrendered without a single person being hurt.

Death of the Prophet

Muhammad returned to live in Madinah, where he led the community both materially and spiritually. In the tenth year after *hijrah*, he fell ill within months of his final pilgrimage to Mecca. After the illness had lasted about two weeks, Muhammad died at the age of sixty-three. By that time, all of Arabia had been united under Islam, and the faith was gaining footholds in other regions.

CHAPTER 6
HINDUISM

Hinduism is a many-faceted faith. For those who enjoy the subtle pleasures of metaphysics, there is the philosophy of monism—that all things, however varied, are Brahman. (Brahman is a complicated concept that we'll discuss in more detail shortly; for now, think of it as "oneness.") Those drawn to lasting moral and political ideas can trace a continuous thread from the nonviolence that runs from the fifth-century B.C. Jains—who believed that no living thing should be harmed—all the way to Mohandas K. Gandhi—who was inspired by the Jains and embraced a philosophy of *ahimsa*, or nonviolence.

For more than 2,000 years, Yoga has taught concentration and meditation techniques as a means to know God. Hinduism created offshoots such as Jainism and Buddhism, which prescribed their own *dharma*, or set of duties, for living a proper life.

In all of the ages of Hindu thought there are kernels of insight. Consider this one: The great king Yudhishthira once said that the most wonderful and truly startling thing in life is that every moment we see people dying around us, and yet we think we shall never die.

For those seeking common ground between Eastern and Western thought, you need only look at the Hindu emphasis on a reality beyond the world of our senses. The following passage is from the ancient Katha Upanishad (3.3–7, 10–14). The metaphor of the chariot here also makes an appearance in Plato as he discusses the virtue of self-control.

> Think of the soul as the master of a chariot. The body is the chariot itself, the faculty of reason is the rider, and the mind is the reins. The senses are the horses, and desires are the roads on which they travel.

> When the master of a chariot has full control of the chariot, the rider, the reins, and the horses, then the chariot moves swiftly and smoothly. In the same way when the soul controls the body, the mind and the senses, life is joyful and happy. But when the master lacks control, the horses run wild. In the same way when the body, the mind and the senses are not controlled by the soul, there is misery and pain.

> The objects of desire guide the senses. The senses supply information to the mind, and so influence what the mind thinks. The thoughts of the mind are ordered by the faculty of reason. And reason only operates successfully when it is guided by the soul. Reason and the mind can be trained to hear the guidance of the soul, and obey it. The training takes the form of meditation, by which the reason and the mind rise to a higher level of consciousness.

> So wake up, rise to your feet, and seek a teacher who can train you.

Plato and the Upanishads started in two different places but arrived at the same truth: Genuine happiness can only be attained when reason steers the desires, not the other way around. The idea is more than 2,500 years old.

THE FOUR AIMS OF LIFE

Atha, Moksha, Kama, and Dharma

Hinduism is a most practical religion, complete with purposes for living. What are these goals? They are presented in a doctrine called the Four Ends of Life. Each of these aims prescribes a value or manner of conduct that is a piece of a larger moral view. Each is therefore appropriate for a proper Hindu upbringing. While the four are emphasized at different stages of life, one reigns above the rest: *dharma*.

Hindu for Life

Recent evidence shows that followers of Hinduism are more likely to stay with their religion than followers of any other major religion. According to a Pew forum poll, 90 percent of all people who are raised Hindu remain Hindu. This ranks first among the major religions, with Catholics (89 percent) and Jewish people (85 percent) running second and third.

At times, Hindu texts reduce our aspirations to three: *dharma* (virtue), material gain, and love or pleasure. Dharma provides the underpinning for the others, for the concept of dharma establishes an ideal of behavior, religion, and ethics. If we are living appropriately at the various stages of life, we are always doing our dharma.

The Ultimate Goal

Hinduism teaches that the ultimate goal of life is to keep from being reborn. It is only by transcending selfishness that one can achieve that destiny. According to the classic text The Bhagavad Gita, the way to the cessation of the cycle of rebirth is to perform all of our actions just because such actions are our dharma, without egotistical concern for their fruits.

Even those who live large lives of outsized pleasure are called upon to follow the duties of dharma. Kings must observe dharma and enforce it among their subjects. A king who follows the injunctions of dharma is called a royal sage, for his rule is based on moral principles. The *Lawbook of Yajnavalkya* states that where there is a conflict between righteousness and material advantage, dharma and *artha*, dharma comes first.

Moksha is last in the Hindu scheme of values, for it ought to be the final and supreme aspiration of man. In a well-lived life, young boys and girls attend to accomplishments like learning; in youth, enjoyment should be the principle aim; in later life, one should pursue the ideals of virtue and spiritual liberation. *Moksha* is this desire to be free of the endless cycle of transmigration that traps the spirit.

Artha

Artha signifies material prosperity and achieving worldly well-being. The word signifies the whole range of tangible objects that can be possessed, enjoyed, and lost, and which we require in our lives for the upkeep of a household, raising of a family, and discharge of religious duties. Wealth and material well-being is not its own end; rather, it is a means to an enriched life.

Successes in the stage of artha help us support a household and discharge our civic duties. But there are limitations: Success here is private, not cooperative. There is another problem: Wealth, fame, and power do not survive death and are, therefore, ephemeral.

Kama

Kama, the second aim of life, has to do with fun, but more generally, pleasure. In Indian mythology, Kama is the counterpart of Cupid; he is the Hindu god of love. Kama refers to the emotional being of a person, their feelings and desires.

According to Indian philosophy, people who are denied their emotional lives and the fulfillment of pleasurable desires are repressed and live under a continual strain. All of this is ruinous to their sanity and well-being.

Seek Pleasure, Avoid Pain

Hinduism acknowledges that seeking pleasures and avoiding pain is fundamental to human psychology, and therefore pleasure is one of the ends—or goals—of existence. But people do come to the realization that pleasure is not all there is. In fact, the nonstop pursuit of pleasure is rather trivial and ultimately boring; people desire something more lasting.

The principal surviving classic of India's kama teaching is Vatsayana's celebrated *Kama Sutra*. The work is more or less a textbook for lovers and courtesans. In an environment of arranged marriages, there were plenty of dull and painful households where a perusal of the *Kama Sutra* would come in handy.

Dharma

The third of the four aims, dharma, includes, in essence, the sum and substance of the religious and moral duties that comprise our righteousness. Indian literature contains rituals and numerous social regulations of the three upper castes—Brahmin (priest), Kshatriya (noble), and Vaishya (merchant and agriculturalist)—meticulously formulated according to the teaching of the Creator himself (in the Vedas).

Dharma is the doctrine of the duties and rights of each group and person in the ideal society, and as such, the law or mirror of all moral action. Ethical life is the means to spiritual freedom, as well as its expression on earth. At this stage, the individual directs his energy toward helping others, but this service is also finite and so will come to an end.

Moksha

What people really want is found in the fourth aim, which is spiritual release. The chief end of humanity is the full development of the individual. The Upanishad tells us that there is nothing higher than people, but people are not mere assemblages of body, life, and mind born of and subject to physical nature.

The natural half-animal being is not a person's whole or real being; it is but the instrument for the use of spirit that is the truth of their being. It is the ultimate aim, the final good, and as such is set over and above the other three. Artha, kama, and dharma are the pursuits of the world; each implies its own orientation or life philosophy, and to each a special literature is dedicated.

THE VEDAS

The Wisdom of the Hindu Scriptures

Veda is a Sanskrit word meaning "wisdom" or "knowledge." These were the oldest scriptures of Hinduism and also the most authoritative of the Hindu sacred texts. In fact, all later texts are considered to be mere commentary on the Vedas. For Hindus, they are the basic source for understanding the universe.

The Vedas developed from a group of sages and *rishis* (in the Vedic sense, a seer or inspired poet), who discovered the truths and realities that lie behind human existence and formulated a set of rules for good living. These rules, known as dharma and anti-dharma (*adharma*), are components of Hinduism. They are eternal truths and applicable to all times. The Vedas are highly developed mythology. These sacred texts are divided into two groups—*sruti* (revealed) and *smriti* (remembered)—and were kept by people through oral tradition, from one generation to the next.

Age of the Vedas

Estimates about the time the Vedas were written vary widely, with some scholars maintaining they were recorded prior to 2000 B.C., before the arrival of the Aryans, and were still being developed as late as the sixth century B.C. Other estimates contend that the Vedas were composed anywhere from 1500 to 400 B.C.

The four basic collections of Vedas are the Rigveda, Yajurveda, Samaveda, and Atharayaveda.

The Four Vedas

The earliest written document is the Rigveda, a collection of 1,017 Sanskrit poems addressed to various gods, as well as three other collections (*samhitas*)—the Sama, Yajur, and Atharva Vedas—a collection of hymns used in the ritual services, all written in archaic poetic texts.

The Rigveda, also known as the Veda of Verses, is the first portion of the Vedas and consists of 1,028 hymns covering 10,600 stanzas of praise to the nature gods, particularly Agni—the fire god—and Indra—the warrior god.

The purpose of the Vedas was to teach people their dharma—their conduct and duty in the present life. The Vedas are also used for sacrifices. These hymns are to be intoned with special tunes, and the pronunciations of the words must be accurate, since they are addressed to special gods thanking the deities and asking for material favors.

Gods and Nature

In the Vedic cosmology, the universe is divided into three parts—earth, atmosphere, and heaven—and the gods are assigned to these parts. The gods mentioned in the Rigveda are related to forces of nature: Varuna is related to the heavens; Usha is the goddess of dawn; and Surya is related to the sun. Indra is the most important of all atmospheric gods.

In later years, commentaries on these hymns, called Brahmanas, were written. Still later, in the sixth century B.C., mystical philosophical works were developed that differed from previous Bramanas and Samhitas. These works are called Vedanta Upanishads. The Bhagavad Gita (a later addition to the Upanishads) and the Upanishads themselves form the basis for the sacred scriptures of Hinduism. The Vedas and Upanishads are the foremost scriptures in antiquity, both in authority and importance. Other major scriptures include the *Tantras*, the sectarian *Agamas*, the *Puranas* (legends), and the epics *Mahabharata* and *Ramayana*.

The Yajurveda, the Samaveda, and the Atharvaveda

The Rigveda is the most important, but the other three Vedas are also significant. Each of the Vedic books is subdivided into four parts. Each contains a section of hymns to the gods, which recall the period when statements about the gods were memorized, chanted, and passed on from one generation to another; ritual instructions (Brahmanas), in which worshipers are given instructions about how to perform their sacrifices; the so-called Forest Treatises (Aranyakas), which give instructions to hermits in their religious pursuits; and the Upanishads, composed of philosophical materials.

Again, it is believed that the Vedas were revealed to the sages by God. The other possibility is that the Vedas revealed themselves to the seers or *mantradrasta* of the hymns. The Vedas were compiled by Vyasa Krishma Dwaipayana around the time of the Lord Krishna, around 1500 B.C. Just as the gospels have four writers, there are four primary seers—Atri, Kanwa, Vashistha, and Vishwamitra.

The Yajurveda

The Yajurveda, known as the Veda of Sacrificial Texts, is a collection of sacrificial rites. Simply put, it is a liturgical collection including the materials to be recited during sacrifices to the gods.

The Yajurveda serves as a practical guidebook for the priests who execute sacrificial acts, simultaneously muttering the prose prayers and the sacrificial formulae (*yajus*). It is similar to ancient Egypt's *Book of the Dead*.

The Yajurveda inspires humans to walk on the path of karma (deeds), so it is also called Karmaveda. It comprises hymns taken from the Rigveda and adds explanatory notes in prose form. It contains fifty chapters each, which are subdivided into *kandikas*, or paragraphs, numbering 1,975 mantras.

The Samaveda

The third book, the Samaveda, is also known as the Veda of Chants or Book of Songs. It contains the required melodies and chants recited by priests for special sacrifices. It is a collection of spiritual hymns, used as musical notes, which were almost completely drawn from the Rigveda and have no distinctive lessons of their own.

Most of the Samaveda's mantras are taken from the Rigveda, but the order is modified for chanting. It is divided into two books called *ankas*. It has twenty-one chapters and contains 1,875 mantras. These mantras are addressed to Agni, Indra, and Sama.

The Atharvaveda

The Atharvaveda is the Veda of the Fire Priest, consisting of occult formulas and spells. This Book of Spells, the last of the Vedas, is completely different from the other three Vedas and is next in importance to Rigveda with regard to history and sociology.

Its hymns are of a more diverse character than the Rigveda and are simpler in language. In fact, many scholars do not consider it part of the Vedas at all. This Veda consists of spells and charms prevalent at the time it was written, and it portrays a clearer picture of the Vedic society.

THE UPANISHADS

God Is One with Many Forms

The Upanishads are the fourth section of each of the Vedas. The word *Upanishads* means "sitting near," as in being near enough to listen to your sage or master. The conversations in the Upanishads took place between gurus and their students as they sat and ruminated over the philosophical implications of the Vedas.

Religion 101 Question

How many Upanishads are there?

There are currently about 200 Upanishads, ranging in length from one to fifty pages. About fourteen, or less than 10 percent, of these are known as principle Upanishads. The earliest likely originated in the ninth century B.C.

The following are the main ideas expounded in the Upanishads:

- God is one, without a second, absolute and indivisible. God assumes various personal forms to reveal himself to us.
- All of the incarnations (manifestations of God on Earth) are actual embodiments of Divinity.
- There are no accidents in the cosmic universe; human destiny is governed by the law of cause and effect.
- We are born on earth repeatedly to finish the unfinished work of realizing our divinity.

- There is a higher state of consciousness that can be achieved in this human birth.
- There are many ways to achieve union with God: through the intellect, emotions, actions, and the will.

A dominating theme of the Upanishads seems to be the ultimate identity of Brahman (wholeness; unity) and atman (self). However, there are other ways to interpret the relationship between the two principles. One of the Upanishads, Svetasvatara, speaks of Brahman as God, making a distinction between this and the external world. In addition to this theistic interpretation, there is also a tendency toward pantheism, a tendency to think of the natural universe and the individual soul as God.

The Nature of the Upanishads

The Upanishads are more philosophical and mystical in character than the Vedas. In the Upanishads, scholars observe for the first time a concept of a single, supreme God (Brahman) who is knowable by the human self (*atman*).

Another school of thought disagrees, saying that polytheism pervades the earlier Vedic material, with its stress on the proper manner of worshiping many gods. By way of contrast, the Upanishads are monistic; that is, all reality is one, not many. This reality is an impersonal being known as Brahman. All other entities that exist in nature—and even beyond nature—are a manifestation of this omnipresent Brahman. Trees, sky, earth, water, spiritual entities—all things material and immaterial are not diverse, but express a single reality: Brahman.

Salt in Water

A verse in the Upanishads illustrates the oneness of the universe: "When a chunk of salt is thrown into water, it dissolves into that very water, and it cannot be picked up in any way. Yet, from whatever place one may take a sip, the salt is there! In the same way this Immense Being has no limit or boundary and is a single mass of perception."

In the way of knowing that pertains to Brahman, the highest kind of knowledge is to recognize that only Brahman is real. By logical implication, all that is not Brahman is unreal. The novice may labor under the illusion that Brahman and the rest of reality are separate. In fact no object, not even our own selves, are separate from Brahman.

This emphasis on philosophy, in this case monism (the belief in the oneness of the universe), sets the Upanishads apart from the Vedas. In the Vedas, the stress was on how to worship the various Aryan gods by means of sacrifice, but the Upanishads emphasize dispassionate meditation on the ultimate nature of reality.

True Knowledge

According to the Upanishads, the proper diagnosis of our human illness is that we live in ignorance (*avidya*) of the true nature of reality. The prescription for this philosophical illness is to arrive at true knowledge. In Hinduism, liberation only comes with right thinking.

Much of this philosophy is a metaphysical search for Brahman, the absolute ground of all being. According to the Upanishads, a single, unifying principle underlies the entire universe. *Brahman* is a Sanskrit word meaning "the eternal, imperishable, absolute." This being is also unknowable and has no past, present, or future. Brahman is also impersonal, not completely unlike the god of the deists at the time of the European Enlightenment. In fact, *Brahman* also means "ever growing."

If we remove all the materials and living things from the universe, strip away all its furniture, and empty it of all being, fullness will still be left behind. That is because even without material objects, there will always be Brahman.

The Shvetashvatara Upanishad emphasizes the idea that separateness is an illusion.

It proceeds as follows:

1 What is the cause of the cosmos? Is it Brahman?

From where do we come? By what live?

Where shall we find peace at last?

What power governs the duality

Of pleasure and pain by which we are driven?

2 Time, nature, necessity, accident,

Elements, energy, intelligence—

None of these can be the First Cause

They are effects, whose only purpose is

To help the self rise above pleasure and pain.

3 In the depths of meditation, sages

Saw within themselves the Lord of Love,

Who dwells in the heart of every creature.

Deep in the hearts of all he dwells, hidden

Behind the gunas of law, energy,

And inertia. He is One. He it is

Who rules over time, space, and causality.

All Is Brahman

The underlying monism of the Upanishads says that all of the living beings that inhabit the world are manifestations of Brahman. These living things bear souls (*atman*) that, when taken together, make up Brahman. The world of senses (tenth stanza) tells us of the separateness of the world. But to see the phenomenal world as separate is to see the world in an illusory fashion. To see Brahman is to see one, not many; to see changeless being, not superficial differences; to see unity, not separation.

Brahman is a state of pure transcendence that cannot be grasped by thought or speech.

The greatest spiritual ill of human beings is that they fail to recognize reality for what it is. "Those who worship ignorance enter blinding darkness," says the Upanishads.

THE BHAGAVAD GITA

Song of the Blessed Lord

Bhagavad Gita means "song of the blessed lord," and is sometimes translated as "the song of the adorable one." Believed to have been composed between the second and third century, it is an epic poem of Indian culture and religion. It is to Hinduism what the Homeric poems are to Greek and Hellenistic culture. Like those Homeric poems, the Gita is about a great battle. Through stories of the struggles of notable heroes and gods, it relays much of the basic philosophy of life and states the guiding principles of yoga. The main theme is yoga—the attainment of union with the divine. Krishna distinguishes three forms of yoga: knowledge, action, and devotion.

The Bhagavad Gita is part of a segment of a longer poem called the *Mahabharata*, which is the story of the struggles between two leading families from the beginning of Indian history. These two families face off in the battle of Kurukshetra, which historians place between 850 and 650 B.C.

The Gita begins when the hero, Arjuna, a warrior, hesitates over entering into battle against members of his own family. Arjuna's conscience revolts at the thought of the war and the idea that it involves the killing of friends and relatives. He asks his charioteer Krishna to pull the chariot up between the two battling armies. It becomes apparent that the charioteer Krishna is God himself. The conversation is a revelation given by a friend to a friend, a young god to his companion, the prince Arjuna.

Religion 101 Question

Is there a philosophy of karma in the Bhagavad Gita?

Yes, though the meaning of karmic action has changed from earlier texts. Krishna reveals to Arjuna that action performed out of a sense of one's duty or dharma, with no thought of selfish gain, leads to spiritual fulfillment.

In the course of the conversation, Krishna begins a lecture on the nature of reality. He sets out to outline several yogas that will help Arjuna fight the battle. Krishna is not only playing the part of spiritual advisor to his friend, he is also using this moment to proclaim to all mankind his doctrine of salvation for the world. His doctrine, known as the "Yoga of Selfless Action" (*karma yoga*), entails self-surrender and devotion (*bhakti*) to the Lord, who is identical with the Self within all.

Krishna instructs Arjuna about the nature of reality. The things of this world are not lasting, are unreal, and men are too attached to the things of the senses.

These attachments include the impermanent pleasures and pain of their own bodies.

> *If any man thinks he slays, and if another thinks he is slain, neither knows the ways of truth. The Eternal in man cannot kill: the Eternal in man cannot die.*

> *He is never born and never dies. He is in Eternity: he is for evermore. Never-born and eternal, beyond times gone or to come, he does not die when the body dies.*

What then, Arjuna asks, is the nature of wisdom? Krishna replies:

> *When a man puts away all the desires of his mind, O Arjuna, and when his spirit is content in itself, then he is called stable in intelligence.*

> *He whose kind is untroubled in the midst of sorrows and is free from eager desire amid pleasures, he from whom passion, fear, and rage have passed away, he is called a sage of settled intelligence.*

> *He who is without affection on any side, who does not rejoice or loathe as he obtains good or evil, his intelligence is firmly set in wisdom.*

Now Krishna instructs Arjuna in the manner of selfless action. The unselfish man does an action not for its consequences or rewards, but out of devotion and for the action itself. Indeed, the Bhagavad Gita recommends that the way to escape meaningless cycles of rebirth is to perform all one's actions without egotistical concern for their fruits.

Moderation in All Things

The Bhagavad Gita presents what might be called a "prescriptive ethic," ordering a way of life for the common man. In fact, it doesn't require that one be austere in physical or mental discipline; a yoga that required such extreme behavior was beyond the reach of the common man. The Gita has but one prescription for self-discipline— temperate behavior.

Krishna explains that all that is required is self-control.

The Spiritual Outlook of the Bhagavad Gita

The Bhagavad Gita is a lengthy discussion on the nature of duty toward others and personal obligations, and it is also rich in metaphysical thought. The poem manages to interweave our yearning to know, to act, and to have faith.

While spirituality deals with matters that are timeless, our ideals must be in accord with the highest ideals of the age; however, these ideals may vary from age to age. So the *yugadharma*, the ideals of the particular age, must be kept in view.

Hindu Time

In Hindu cosmology, a Yuga, or age, is the smallest unit of cosmological time. Four Yugas make up one Mahayuga, or Great Age: the Golden Age (Krita), the Silver Age (Treta Yuga), the Bronze Age (Dvapara Yuga), and the Iron Age (Kali Yuga). We are currently in the Kali Yuga, the most corrupt of the ages.

The message of the Gita is not sectarian or addressed to any school of thought. Rather, it is universal in scope, intended equally for Brahmin or outcaste. "All paths lead to me," the Gita says. Because it possesses such universality, it finds favor with all classes and schools. In the roughly 2,200 years since the Gita was written, India and the world have gone through various processes of change and stagnation, prosperity and decay. No matter; each age has found something relevant to its time in the Gita. It applies to the moral, social, and spiritual problems that afflict each age.

KARMA AND SAMSARA

Action and Rebirth

After the completion of the Upanishads, the interconnected doctrines of karma and samsara became prominent in Hindu thinking and persist even today. Both have to do with a philosophy of action and the results of that action. According to the ethical concept of karma (often spelled *kharma*), the actions or karmas of individuals in their current births shape their lives in their next births. This is connected to reincarnation, or the cycles of lives. Souls are believed to cycle through human or animal lives until they are liberated and merge with a higher reality.

Karma

The Sanskrit word *karma* comes from a root that means "to do or act." The law of karma says that people reap what they sow. In essence, the law of karma is a law of justice that implies that every thought or deed, whether good or bad, counts in determining how a person will be born in his next life on earth.

Actions Have Consequences

The idea of karma is that every thought, word, or deed will influence whether individuals achieve liberation or will have to repeat the cycle of birth and death. Karma might be understood as the spiritual or ethical residue of every action; in other words, beyond its external, visible effects, every action has a deep impact on our spiritual relationship.

At the dawn of Indian philosophy, Indians came to believe that every action and every thought had a consequence, which would show up in the present life or in a succeeding one. Most Indian sects believed karma operated as an automatic moral sanction, ensuring the evildoer suffered and the righteous prospered.

A person with bad karma could suffer being reborn many times into lower castes of humans—or even lower animals—and then could not be released until he or she had been reborn in the Brahmin, or priestly, caste.

Karma and Good Qualities

In our own time, when an individual is described as talented, kind, or intelligent, it is believed they have genetics or their environment to thank. But ancient thinkers preferred to think that a person possessed or lacked particular qualities due to choices she made in past lives.

A person's good qualities were attributed to good actions he had taken in a past life. On the other hand, a person possessing bad qualities was also the product of his past choices. Every thought, word, and action—and even nonaction—was believed to have deep effects on a person's spiritual relationships.

On the one hand, karma stresses recurrence—continual renewal and rebirth. On the other hand, the doctrine of the identity of atman and the Brahman stresses the permanent and unchanging. This apparent contradiction between the two concepts was solved by the understanding that the cycle of rebirth is caused by ignorance of the true nature of the self and the failure to realize that it never changes.

Emancipation becomes, therefore, a process of coming to an awareness of that state of being that is beyond process, the identity of atman and Brahman. To have that intuitive knowledge is to become immortal, for "knowing All, he becomes All."

Samsara

Samsara is the round or cycle of birth and rebirth that all Hindus are subject to in the Hindu worldview. Each person at the time of death possesses a karmic account balance; whether the actions are good or bad determines that agent's future destiny.

The literal meaning of the word *samsara* is "to wander across." It signifies that, in Indian thought, a person's life force does not pass on with the death of the body, but instead wanders across. That is, the life force migrates to another time and body, where it continues to live.

Trust in Krishna

An illustration of the interrelation of the concepts of karma and samsara occurs in the Bhagavad Gita (Chapter IX, verses 30–31). Krishna says: "Even he with the worst karma who ceaselessly meditates on Me quickly loses the effects of his past actions. Becoming a high-souled being, he soon attains perennial peace. Know this for certain: the devotee who puts his trust in me never perishes."

The term *samsara* also finds a home in Jainism and Buddhism. To a Western way of thinking, this is known as reincarnation. Reincarnation carries with it a burden; the agent will have to live through generations over and over again. This is contrary to the goals of Indian religions, which stress that individuals must break the cycle of karma and samsara to be free of the burden of life. This release from life is the goal of life, and is called moksha.

Such spiritual release is only possible when an individual has a true knowledge of the illusion of life and recognizes the unity of atman and Brahman.

Of the relationship between karma and samsara, Paramahanda Yogananda (1893–1952), a yogi who introduced millions of westerners to meditation, is full of insight:

> Various great Jain teachers of India have been called tirthakaras, "ford makers," because they reveal the passage by which bewildered humanity may cross over and beyond the stormy seas of samsara (the karmic wheel, the recurrence of lives and deaths). Samsara (literally, "a flowing with" the phenomenal flux) induces man to take the line of least resistance.

> To become the friend of God, man must overcome the devils or evils of his own karma or actions that ever urge him to spineless acquiescence in the mayic delusions of the world. A knowledge of the iron law of karma encourages the earnest seeker to find the way of final escape from its bonds. Because the karmic slavery of human beings is rooted in the desires of maya-darkened minds, it is with mind control that the yogi concerns himself.

MOHANDAS GANDHI

Apostle of Peaceful Change

Mohandas K. Gandhi (1869–1948) is better known as Mahatma, a title that means "great soul." In his long and accomplished life, Gandhi became the unofficial leader of India. The philosophy of nonviolence, which he embraced and used to protest British rule of India, would become his legacy.

From Gandhi to King

The Reverend Dr. Martin Luther King Jr. embraced Gandhi's interpretation of nonviolence, and it influenced his crusade to bring about social change in the United States. While King was a student at a theological college in 1948, he became convinced that this was one of the most potent weapons available to oppressed people in their struggle for freedom.

Gandhi's view of nonviolence was not a Hindu religious thought, but a political idea. It was a powerful concept, and has been used frequently as a successful technique to resolve conflict since Gandhi proved its effectiveness.

The Method of Nonviolence Is Born

Nonviolence first entered Gandhi's mind as the result of one particular incident.

By age twenty-four, Mohandas Gandhi was a barrister. He passed the London matriculation examination, and after three years, he returned to India. In 1893, he agreed to assist a South African firm in a case. First-class accommodations were purchased for him and he boarded the train at Durban for the overnight journey. But he had not counted on the reaction of his fellow passengers, all of whom were of European descent.

Gandhi's train pulled into Maritzburg, the capital of Natal, and Gandhi related that a white man entered his compartment and "looked me up and down" and "saw that I was a colored man." This disturbed the man, who charged out of the compartment and returned with two officials. Gandhi was ordered to the third-class compartment. He refused to leave, protesting that he had a first-class ticket. The official persisted, Gandhi dug in his heels, and eventually a constable was summoned to forcibly remove Gandhi and his luggage from the train.

In the morning his employer used his influence to get Gandhi reinstated as a first-class passenger. He suffered more abuse on the way to Pretoria. On one leg of the journey, he had to travel by stagecoach, but was not allowed to sit inside with the other passengers. The ordeal gave Gandhi a sense of the conditions of Indians in South Africa and strengthened his resolve to do something about it.

A Leader for Civil Rights

Within a week of his arrival in Pretoria, Gandhi had summoned all the Indians of the city to a meeting. At this time, the Natal legislature was taking up a bill to deny the vote to Indians. Gandhi could not stop the bill from passing, but he drew attention to the grievances of Indians in South Africa. In 1894, he formed the Natal Indian Congress to fight for the rights of Indians, which became a great force in South African politics. In 1897, he was attacked and nearly lynched by a white mob. His response to the incident was more ethical than legalistic, and showed that a change had come over him; he refused to press charges against his aggressors.

In 1906, the Transvaal government passed a measure compelling the colony's Indian population to register. This included a strip search of women in order to identify any birthmarks. In Johannesburg that year, Gandhi held a mass protest. For the first time, he articulated his philosophy of *satyagraha* or "truth force," asking his fellow Indians to oppose the new law using nonviolent methods.

Gandhi's years in South Africa were pivotal for his political and spiritual development. He resided there from 1893 until 1914; he was twenty-four when he arrived and forty-five when he left. He studied the Bhagavad Gita, and he corresponded with and was influenced by the Russian novelist Leo Tolstoy (1828–1910), who cultivated his own interest in Indian philosophy. In addition, he pored over the writings of a philosophical predecessor and kindred spirit, Henry David Thoreau (1817–1862).

Indians Against the British Occupiers

By 1914, at the outbreak of World War I, Gandhi returned to India to bring his political ideas to bear on the Indian struggle for independence. When the British passed the Rowlatt Act in 1919, a measure that allowed the government to imprison Indians without a trial, Gandhi launched his first call for satyagraha or nonviolent disobedience on Indian soil.

On April 13, 1919, the British answered the show of civil disobedience with violence, in what has become known as the Amritsar Massacre. General Reginald Dyer of the British Army gave the order to fire into a large crowd of people who were listening to a speech. The British machine guns killed 379 Indians and wounded

1,137. The firing would have continued, but the British ran out of ammunition.

In 1920, Gandhi was elected president of the All-India Home Rule League; in 1921, he became the head of the Indian National Congress. Now Gandhi practiced a policy of boycotting all foreign-made goods, especially British goods.

Gandhi and Spinning

Aware of the effect of his behavior on that of his fellow Indians, Gandhi could often be found at his spinning wheel, which he used to spin thread for cloth for all his own clothing. He wanted all Indians to use homespun cloth in place of foreign-made fabric. He became the symbol of the Indian independence movement.

The boycott of all things foreign expanded to British education facilities, and even to a refusal to pay taxes. The British quelled the agitation and sentenced Gandhi to six years in prison for sedition. For health reasons, Gandhi served just three years and was released in 1924. By 1928, the British had appointed a constitutional reform commission with no Indians on it. Gandhi countered by launching another nonviolent resistance campaign, this time against the tax on salt.

Gandhi's famous Salt March in 1929 was a campaign against the salt tax levied by the British. This campaign was a piece of political theater, the highlight of which was the 250-mile Dandhi March from Ahmedabad to the seaside village of Dandhi. There, Gandhi made his own salt, a powerful symbolic image.

By 1934, Gandhi resigned as the party leader of the Indian National Congress because he found a lack of commitment to his program of nonviolence as a way of life for the new India by members of the Congress. Jawaharlal Nehru became the new leader; meanwhile, Gandhi devoted himself to the goal of educating rural India. He fought against the institution of Untouchables, and worked to promote the manufacture of homespun clothing and other village-level cottage industries.

Quit India Movement and Independence from Britain

In 1942, Gandhi made the clarion call "do or die"—either we must free India from British rule or die trying. Still, the method was passive resistance, not violence. The resolution to quit India was passed at the Bombay session of the All-India Congress Committee. In response, the British detained Indians and arrested more than 10,000 people. Gandhi fasted, hoping for the release of the prisoners.

By 1946, the prisoners were set free, and the British conferred with the Indian National Congress to make arrangements for India's independence. Gandhi believed in cooperation between the Hindu and Muslim communities in India and maintained relationships without regard to religious affiliation; he did not believe in segregation of the two faiths. Nonetheless, the Indian National Congress agreed to a partition agreement that cleaved two states out of British India: India and Pakistan. The process of partition in August 1947 was very violent—several million people were forced to flee their homes and at least 1 million were slaughtered in communal riots.

Gandhi sought peace between the two religious groups and between the two new countries, but when he visited New Delhi in an attempt to pacify the two communities on January 30, 1948, a gunshot rang out and the champion of nonviolence fell. Nathuram Godse, a Hindu radical who opposed Gandhi's acceptance of Muslims, had pulled the trigger. It was the irony of ironies—the world's greatest champion of nonviolence, killed by a gunshot. As he expired, Gandhi uttered the word "Rama," an Indian word meaning God.

CHAPTER 7
BUDDHISM

Buddhism traces its roots back to the Buddha, a yogi who lived more than 2,500 years ago in northern India. The Buddha discovered a way to live that radically transformed people's lives, starting with his own. His revolutionary insights have withstood the test of time and his methods can still transform lives as they did in ancient India. The Buddha taught mindfulness, kindness, and compassion. Buddhism, the family of religions that evolved from the Buddha's teachings, is one of the great ethical systems for benefit of humanity.

While Buddhism may be considered a nontheistic religion, it transcends religious belief into practical experience. You don't believe in Buddhism, you practice Buddhism. In fact, you don't even need to be a "Buddhist" to practice "Buddhism." You just have to sit down and meditate.

At a time when yoga had enjoyed widespread popularity, the Buddha was a prodigious yogi. He mastered the yogas of his day and then founded a way that could go beyond all suffering. This way also goes beyond words and needs to be experienced for yourself. The good news is that is available right here, right now.

Jane Hirshfield, in the PBS documentary, *The Buddha*, offers an explanation of the Buddha's teachings in seven words: "Everything changes; everything is connected; pay attention." This is a nice condensing of millions of words attributed to the Buddha in the Pali Canon (a collection of Buddhist scriptures).

THE FOUR NOBLE TRUTHS

The World Is Suffering

The Four Noble Truths can be thought of as a medical metaphor. The Buddha often considered himself to be a physician, more so than the founder of a religion, and as a doctor he offered medicine to heal the illness of the human condition.

As a physician, he provided a diagnosis for the human condition (First Noble Truth), a cause for the condition (Second Noble Truth), a prognosis (Third Noble Truth), and a prescription for the treatment (Fourth Noble Truth). *Dharma*—the truth reflected in these teachings—is the medicine. The Four Noble Truths can take you all the way to enlightenment. His teaching was radical and he was concerned people may not be open to or understand his message.

The Buddha's teachings were a pathway to letting go of suffering, freeing oneself from pain. The Buddha knew the only way was the Middle Way. He knew that excessive pleasure—a life built on sensual delight—or excessive pain—such as the life of an ascetic—led to continual suffering with no release from it.

The First Noble Truth: The Truth of Suffering

The world that the Buddha lived in was a world that knew warfare, great poverty, and disease. Life expectancy was short and infant and child mortality was great. But *dukkha* goes beyond these obvious forms of suffering of aging, sickness, and death. It also refers to a pervasive dissatisfaction that colors every moment of life. *Du* of *dukkha* means "bad" and *ka* means "wheel." The Buddha invoked the metaphor of a "bad wheel" to capture the essence of *dukkha*. It is more than suffering. It describes an oxcart whose wheel is off its axle, biasing every movement of the cart. That bumpy dissatisfaction or sense that things are not right captures the more important aspect of *dukkha*.

If *dukkha* is self-inflicted there is a way out of this misery and it is to this possibility that the remainder of the Four Noble Truths point.

What, O Monks, is the Noble Truth of Suffering? Birth is suffering, sickness is suffering, old age is suffering, death is suffering. Pain, grief, sorrow, lamentation, and despair are suffering. Association with what is unpleasant is suffering, disassociation from what is pleasant is suffering. Not to get what one wants is suffering.
—The Buddha

The Three Marks of Existence

Dukkha is the first of the three marks of existence. *Dukkha* is descriptive; it's the diagnosis. The second two marks are part of the diagnosis. *Anicca* is best translated as "impermanence." Things are constantly changing.

Religion 101 Question

Do I need to isolate myself to realize enlightenment?

The Buddha believed the Path was for everyone and no matter who you are you can realize *nirvana*. Sometimes the most challenging practice takes place in the outside world as you are forced to work harder when confronted with the many distractions of daily life. Enlightenment may be easier in a monastery, but is available anywhere.

Anatta is the next mark and means "no-self" or "not self." *Anatta* suggests that what appears to be "me" is not something solid, enduring, or stable. Whatever this "me," it is also subject to *anicca*. It's always changing from one moment to the next and only gives the appearance of solidity. The Buddha rejects the idea of an eternal soul. Whatever this self appears to be it is not solid and is always changing.

The Three Poisons

The unawakened mind is inextricably intertwined with three poisons:

1. Greed (craving, desire, thirst)
2. Hatred (aversion, aggression)
3. Delusion (ignorance)

They arise out of misunderstanding the three marks of *dukkha*, *anicca*, and *anatta* and, in turn, greed, hatred, and delusion are the primary cause of *dukkha*. In awakening you greatly reduce your involvement with these poisons and it is by reducing these poisons that you can progress toward the awakened mind.

The Five Aggregates

In order to understand the nature of the self, the Buddha broke down the individual into five groups or aggregates of attachment.

The five aggregates he named are as follows.

1. The aggregate of matter (eye, ear, nose, throat, hand, etc.).
2. The aggregate of feelings and sensations (sight, sound, smell, taste, thought, form).
3. The aggregate of perception.

4. The aggregate of volitions or mental formations.
5. The aggregate of consciousness (response).

Each aggregate is subject to change. Your body changes constantly. In fact, most cells of your body change every seven years and, in fact, every atom in your body changes over about once every year. Feelings and sensations change constantly as well. Your ideas change. Your intentions change; these are the basis for your actions.

Since you cannot act on that which you do not experience (you do not act on a sound you do not hear), the fifth aggregate, consciousness, depends on all the other aggregates for its existence. The action or response you make based on the intention you had based on your perception of your senses from your body is *solely* dependent on each of the preceding phenomena. This is the Buddha's teaching of *dependent origination*.

These five aggregates together comprise *duhkha*, or suffering. If you think of a river you will notice that the river is constantly changing. You cannot see one part of the river and stop to examine it and find it as fixed. Just like the river, you are ever changing.

The Second Noble Truth: The Cause of Suffering Is Desire

The Second Noble Truth can be summed up in one word: *desire*, and is known as the truth of arising (of suffering). Desire is like an overflowing river carrying you away to *samsara*.

> *The teaching of Buddha*
> *is like a great cloud*
> *which with a single kind of rain*
> *waters all human flowers*
> *so that each can bear its fruit.*
> —Lotus Sutra 5

You suffer because you reach out for certain things, push other things away, and generally neglect to appreciate that everything is changing constantly (*anicca*). The Buddha calls upon you to examine your relationship to your senses. Are they pushing you around, leading you into trouble, becoming an excessive preoccupation? Find the middle way, neither indulging in nor avoiding sensory experiences.

The Third Noble Truth: Suffering Can End!

Nirvana literally means "cooling by blowing" or "blowing out." What blows out? Adherence to the three poisons (*kleshas*): greed, hatred, and delusion. The misery can stop if life can be approached with wisdom (*Prajna*) instead of desire. With meditation you can see into the three marks of existence and are no longer fooled by them: *dukkha* (suffering; pervasive dissatisfaction), *anicca* (impermanence), and *anatta* (no-self). Advanced meditation provides the opportunity to burn up past karma or the conditionings that you have experienced. It is akin to untying knots that have accumulated in your mind over a lifetime of experiences. Each knot that is untied, each conditioning that is deconditioned, every bit of karma that is burned up moves you closer to awakening.

The Fourth Noble Truth: The Way

To get to nirvana, you must traverse the Noble Eightfold Path (more about this in the following section). This path can be divided into three sections: morality (*sila*; right speech, right action, right livelihood), meditation (*samadhi*; right effort, right mindfulness, right concentration), and wisdom and insight (*Prajna*; right view, right thought). This is an entirely self-sufficient path. No outside intercessor is required to reach this salvation.

This, O Monks, is the Truth of the Path which leads to the cessation of suffering. It is this Noble Eightfold Path, which consists of:

1. Right View
2. Right Resolve
3. Right Speech
4. Right Action
5. Right Livelihood
6. Right Effort
7. Right Mindfulness
8. Right Meditation

—The Truth of the Path (*Magga*)

The Four Noble Truths are the basic teachings of the Buddha. They embody action and have the potential to guide you toward a radical transformation. These teachings revolutionized the spiritual and later political landscape of ancient India. These simple truths are not abstractions. Each one is testable through your own experience. To work through the Four Noble Truths, you recognize, realize experience, and practice. These are the actions for enlightened living. The Four Noble Truths are a wake-up call to how your life is being encumbered with self-inflicted misery and offers a way out of this misery.

THE EIGHTFOLD PATH

The Middle Way

The Middle Way, or the Noble Eightfold Path, is the roadmap for Buddhist living. There are three sections of the Path that contain the eight "right" or "wise" ways to be, and each section is a platform for the next in a continuous process.

The Path
1. Right Action
2. Right Speech
3. Right Livelihood
4. Right Effort
5. Right Concentration
6. Right Mindfulness
7. Right View
8. Right Resolve

The Buddha uses the word *right* in the way we would say something is appropriate. The Buddha is not prescribing or proscribing specific actions because appropriate action depends on context. These right approaches stem from directly experiencing which actions lead to happiness and which actions lead to misery.

The Eightfold Path is divided into three categories. They are:

1. Morality (*Sila*)
2. Meditation (*Samadhi*)
3. Wisdom (*Prajna*)

Morality includes numbers one, two, and three: right speech, right action, and right livelihood. Meditation is made up of the middle three steps (four, five, and six): right effort, right concentration, and right mindfulness. And finally, Wisdom is comprised of numbers seven and eight: right view and right resolve.

Practice, Practice

The eight steps are not meant to be done sequentially but are to be practiced all the time, simultaneously, each and every one. The Middle Way is a program of action.

Right Speech

Speech is a powerful force and can be used for good or for harm. To practice right speech, you must speak the truth and avoid unnecessary communications such as gossip. While you might not always be certain of the right thing to say, you probably know the *wrong* things to say:

- Lies
- Slander
- Cursing or abusive language
- Raising one's voice unnecessarily
- Harsh words
- Speaking too much (rattling on)
- Gossip
- Creating enmity

Right Action

Right action can be understood through the directive "Do no harm," at least not intentionally. Right action is similar to right speech. Your actions should be harmonious with your environment leading to peace rather than ill will. Do nothing that will cause harm to others. Obviously harmful acts include the following:

- Stealing
- Taking of life, human and otherwise
- Destruction of person or property or peacefulness
- Overindulging

Right action includes sexual responsibility—no adultery or prostitution. It also includes abstaining from alcohol and recreational drugs.

Right Livelihood

Right livelihood means to avoid harm through your work in the world. Just as with sensory perceptions of the body, the goal is not renunciation, but rather a lack of attachment. There is no prohibition against the accumulation of wealth or of having luxurious possessions. It all depends on the relationship you have to these things.

Occupations a Buddhist might want to avoid include but are not limited to the following:

- Arms dealer
- Drug dealer
- Working with intoxicants and poisons
- Butcher
- Executioner

Religion 101 Question

Where did the name for the Lotus 1-2-3 computer program come from?

Mitch Kapor, computer programmer and developer of the program, is a practicing Buddhist. In Buddhism, the lotus flower symbolizes the purity of mind, body, and spirit floating above the muddy waters of attachment.

Right Effort

The next three disciplines are all mental disciplines and directly relate to meditation practices.

All this practice takes quite a bit of effort, so now you need to make sure you are using the appropriate amount of effort, somewhere in between the extremes of laziness and overdoing it. Right effort also means getting rid of improper attitudes and thoughts. When unproductive or unsavory thoughts arise you must expend the necessary level of effort to return your attention to what is happening in the present moment.

Right Concentration

As mentioned earlier, progress along the Path requires meditation. The mind must be your ally and not your enemy. The Buddha did not invent meditation; such techniques were being practiced in his day and for thousands of years before his time. As a child, the Buddha was a meditation prodigy, falling into a meditative state spontaneously under the Rose Apple Tree when he was eight years old.

Mindfulness was the method that most directly spoke to the impermanence of things and helped the Buddha to realize his awakening.

Right concentration is an important foundation for right mindfulness. It is by practicing the appropriate forms of concentration that you make mindfulness more available.

Right Mindfulness

Right mindfulness requires a foundation of right concentration. While practicing mindfulness meditation or *vipassana* you will have a direct experience of the three marks of existence. By paying attention to, for instance, the rising and falling of your breathing or the arising and fading away of sensations in the body, you will have a direct experience of impermanence (*anicca*). When you see how your mind engages with painful stories or identifies with themes of loss or deprivation, you have a direct experience of suffering (*dukkha*). When you practice and the mind gets concentrated and stays with the moment-to-moment phenomenological energies of being alive you have a direct experience of no-self (*anatta*).

Right mindfulness asks you to retrieve your attention from the future, especially if that future-oriented attention takes the form of worry. Right mindfulness asks you to retrieve your attention from the past, especially if that past-oriented attention takes the form of regret. Once retrieved, bring your attention back to the present moment and notice with interest what is happening.

Right View

Right view means to have a total comprehension of the Four Noble Truths. Right thought means a detachment from hatred (and cruelty). These factors are unique to the Buddha's teachings. The culmination of these views, based on morality and meditation, is the experience of Prajna (wisdom or insight into the ultimate reality of things).

We are what we think. All that we are arises with our thoughts.
With our thoughts, we make our world.
—The Buddha

What did the Buddha mean by right view? Right view is the ability to experience things beyond conditioned experience. It removes the biasing filters of past experience and allows you to experience reality closer to the way it actually is. It requires letting go of preconceptions, judgments, and reactivity developed over a lifetime of habit. Meditation (and its constituents, right effort, concentration, and mindfulness) will help you to identify your preconceptions, judgments, and reactivity, and to see how they are active in your experience.

The Eight Hooks

The Buddha warns about the eight worldly things to avoid. These four pairs of opposites are:

1. Taking delight in money, material possessions; feeling distress when separated from these things.
2. Taking delight in praise and things that boost the ego; feeling distress when receiving criticism or disapproval.
3. Taking delight in maintaining a good reputation or personal image; feeling distress when image and reputation are diminished.
4. Taking delight when making contact with pleasurable things; feeling distress when making contact with unpleasurable things.

These are eight attitudes that make you vulnerable to *dukkha* (suffering; pervasive dissatisfaction, and so forth). The Buddha is not encouraging you to become zombie-like with no self-preserving instincts. Rather, he is cautioning against basing your self-worth, happiness, and well-being on their occurrence.

In other words, beware of contingent self-worth. All things mentioned here are either not in your direct control (that is, it is something someone else does to us) or they cannot be controlled because they are always changing (that is, the fundamental truth of impermanence).

Right Resolve

Right resolve involves intentions. The spirit in which you approach everything—a spirit of kindness, compassion, and harmlessness to your fellow beings—is essential to right resolve. The goal is to move away from the ego-related concerns of "me" and "mine," toward a lifestyle of service where your motivations are not ego-driven but more selfless.

A Noble Process

The Noble Eightfold Path is a process. Don't worry about getting it perfectly at every moment. The Path provides the methods to rid the believer of negative emotions and replace suffering with acceptance.

THE THREE JEWELS

The Spiritual Heart of Buddhism

You might call yourself a Buddhist if you practice the Five Precepts and if you take refuge in the Three Jewels. But what is meant by the Three Jewels of Buddhism? The Three Jewels are the basic components of Buddhist belief. They are:

- The *Buddha*
- The *Dharma*
- The *Sangha*

Buddha means the Awakened One. The Enlightened One. For the *buddha* jewel you take the *buddha* as your refuge—not the person of that Buddha but the possibility for awakening. The Buddha taught that everyone has *buddhanature*, that is, the capacity to awaken. You are *buddha*, and it is to this realization that refuge is taken.

Dharma has multiple meanings. *Dharma* is the collection of the Buddha's teachings. In the Buddha's time wandering ascetics would meet each other and ask, "Whose *dharma* do you follow?" They would then provide the name of their teacher. The Buddha was unique in that he did not follow another teacher's *dharma* but had figured things out for himself under the pipal tree. *Dharma* also refers to the deeper truths that the Buddha's teachings point to. It refers to the truth of *dukkha* and the possibility of *nirvana*. *Dharma* is also translated as "natural law"; seeing clearly into the reality of things.

Equally important is the community, the *sangha*. The early *sangha* was comprised of the Buddha and his followers. This included his five formerly ascetic friends and the proliferation of people that followed including common people and kings. People joined the community through their wish to end suffering and upon hearing the wisdom of the Buddha. You could become a monastic or be part of the community as a lay practitioner.

Twenty-five hundred years later, these choices are still available and the *sangha* is one of humanity's oldest continuous institutions.

Yet, it is not a formal community. It has no central authority, holds no annual conference, and has no membership roster. It is a loosely collected group of like-minded individuals who practice living the Four Noble Truths and other Buddhist teachings, practices, and rituals that have developed over the centuries. The *sangha* is the worldwide collection of Buddhist practitioners as well as the small group of people with whom you meet to meditate together on a regular basis in your community. Even individuals who practice on their own are part of the *sangha*.

When we say, "I take refuge in the Buddha," we should also understand that "The Buddha takes refuge in me," because without the second part the first part is not complete. The Buddha needs us for awakening, understanding, and love to be real things and not just concepts. They must be real things that have real effects on life. Whenever I say, "I take refuge in the Buddha," I hear "Buddha takes refuge in me."

—Thich Nhat Hanh, *Being Peace*

Monks and Nuns

In the East, there is a long tradition of monastic orders or monks (*bikkhu*) and nuns (*bhikkunis*). To become a monk or nun is to devote yourself to spiritual life and the Three Jewels. A child is old enough to become a monk when he can "scare the crows away," which usually means about seven or eight years old. Life for a monk is simple. Monks and nuns are expected to shave their heads and live a life of celibacy.

Monasteries can be quite elaborate and large social institutions. For example, the Abhayagiri monastery in fifth-century Sri Lanka had 5,000 monks. Prior to China's invasion of Tibet in 1959, the Drepung monastery housed 10,000 monks.

The First Jewel: The Buddha

The Buddha was both a man and a symbol. When you take refuge in the Buddha you bow in respect to what this man accomplished in his lifetime. When you take refuge in the Buddha you also bow to what he represents—your awakened nature.

Some people, especially in traditional Buddhist cultures, may look to Buddha as a source of salvation. In Tibet he is referred to as Lord Buddha. In the West, however, he is more the hero of an epic story of sacrifice and deliverance from greed, hatred, and delusion. He had everything, then nothing before finding the Middle Way. Through his voluminous teaching over a long career he has left a detailed path that any interested party can follow. He left a repertoire of methods that can lead to liberation. He was a great yogi and represents the potential for radical transformation, from a life of suffering to a life of liberation.

Buddhanature—the Buddha within everyone—is not created but rather revealed. It is present now, but perhaps obscured by your stories of desire and aversion. Buddhanature is not made; it is not a destination. It is here right now. The Buddha showed humanity this potential.

The Fat "Buddha"

The fat and happy "Buddha" you've seen in Chinese restaurants is not Siddhartha Gautama, Shakyamuni Buddha. He is Budai in China or Hotei in Japan. He is often depicted smiling and laughing. He is more of a folklore figure, but is often mistaken for the historical Buddha.

The Buddha does not ask you to believe in him or to pray to him. Any peace of mind that comes to you comes from your own effort and not divine intervention. He shows us a path that we are free to take all on our own.

The Second Jewel: The *Dharma*

The second of the Three Jewels is the *dharma*. The *dharma* is the entire collection of Buddhist scripture and thought, including all modern Buddhist teachings, as well as the traditional, original teachings, such as the *sutras* in the Pali Canon. The *dharma* is all the spoken word and written text passed down through the generations.

Today there are many sources for the *dharma*: books, DVDs, MP3s, streaming Internet video, and recorded *dharma* talks. There are also practice centers and monasteries. The proliferation of Buddhism in the West in conjunction with modern communication technologies has created an unprecedented availability of the *dharma*.

There are two types of *dharma*: that which can be read or heard—transmitted from person to person—and that which is realized. *Realized dharma* is *dharma* experienced through the practice of the Four Noble Truths—the realization of the Truth, or awakening.

The Third Jewel: The *Sangha*

The Buddha's first followers were his five formerly ascetic colleagues. Soon, though, he went from teaching men who were already renunciants to lay people. A wealthy young man named Yashas became a follower and attained enlightenment under the Buddha's tutelage. Yashas's father also became a follower but as a lay practitioner (*upsaka*). Lay followers did not follow monastic rules, but practiced the teaching by taking the Triple Refuge: Buddha, *Dharma, Sangha*. Yashas's mother also took refuge in the Triple Jewel and became the first female lay follower. Friends of Yashas came, and friends of friends. Word spread. The Buddha sent the first sixty enlightened ones out to spread the teachings.

Religion 101 Question

Can the average person attain enlightenment?

Vacchagotta approached the Buddha and asked him if there were lay followers practicing the Buddha's principles who achieved "high spiritual states." The Buddha told Vacchagotta that yes, there were "not one or two, not a hundred or two hundred or five hundred but many more" who did.

Despite the Buddha's repudiation of the caste system, not everyone was welcome in the *sangha*. If you were a debtor, a criminal, runaway slave, or other person shunned by society, you were not welcome. The Buddha likely made such rules mindful of not offending his wealthy patrons upon whose generosity the *sangha* depended. In this way, he was a skilled politician and not detached from the practical realities of life. The *sangha* depended upon the patronage of kings and the wealthy. To this end accommodations were made. The most controversial issue where the Buddha did depart from social norms was allowing women to be ordained as nuns (*bikkhunis*). It took some repeated pleading, however, from his Aunt Prajapati.

Generosity

Dana (donation) is a key Buddhist practice throughout the world. Giving generates a sense of generosity that is an antidote to the poison of greed. Giving also helps the practitioner to cultivate a sense of compassion for others and to overcome selfishness and the notion of an enduring self.

There would be no Buddhism today without the generosity of kings, merchants, and common people at the time of the Buddha and beyond. Giving results in merit, but the giving cannot be calculated solely to attain merit; giving should be done with serene joy.

Merit can also be transferred to others, such that your generous acts could be offered for the benefit of all humanity. In Tibet, for instance, family members of the deceased will offer merit to assist in a favorable rebirth. Even kings took this seriously. For example, Sri Lankan kings would keep "merit books" of all their good deeds and have these read back to them on their deathbeds to put their minds at ease.

THERAVADA, MAHAYANA, AND VAJRAYANA BUDDHISM

The Jewel Has Many Facets

There is no one Buddhism; no essential Buddhism that can be taken apart from its tradition. In fact, the term *Buddhism* is a relatively recent invention, first coined by scholars in the eighteenth and nineteenth centuries. Prior to this Buddhists were called "followers of the Buddha."

There are three different vehicles, or schools, of Buddhist teachings, and virtually all sects of Buddhism fall into one of these three schools. Theravada and Mahayana Buddhism grew out of the early councils as differences arose in practice and philosophy. The three vehicles of Buddhism are:

1. Theravada
2. Mahayana
3. Vajrayana

These vehicles, while overlapping, can be considered distinct religions.

What's It Mean?

The word *vehicle* comes from the Sanskrit word *vada*, meaning "ferryboat." Think of the image of the river crosser and his raft; these vehicles can ferry you across the river of samsara to nirvana.

There is no one authority on Buddhism—there is no pope, no president, no leader of the Buddhist people. There is no central office, no definitive source. Buddhism is alive in many forms, with many voices today. Within the three vehicles there are Tibetan Buddhism, Zen Buddhism, Pure Land, Yogacara, and more. But all these forms can fit within the three vehicles, and some would agree that they could even fit within the two main vehicles—Theravada and Mahayana.

Theravada Versus Mahayana

Mahayana Buddhism emerged as a reaction to early Buddhist orthodoxies in the first century, although the term *Mahayana* does not appear until the sixth century. Mahayana took root in northern India and made its way east and north to Tibet, Mongolia, China, and Japan. Mahayana diverges philosophically with Theravada and claims to be based on texts attributable to the Buddha that are not in the Pali Canon and were not discovered until centuries after the death of the Buddha.

On the one hand, Mahayana offers the possibility of becoming a buddha to everyone and on the other hand elevates the Buddha from a compassionate teacher to a celestial guru. Such "buddha realms" or "pure lands" may be taken literally or metaphorically to represent certain states of being. Devotion to your teacher is also a key feature of Mahayana traditions such as Zen and Vajrayana, where your teacher is seen as the living embodiment of Buddha, providing you with the opportunity to become Buddha, too. Consequently, there is more emphasis on lineage.

Well awake they arise, at all times,
The disciples of Gautama,
In whom both day and night,
Constantly there is mindfulness on the Buddha.
—Dhammapada

The Mahayana placed more emphasis on the *bodhisattva* and de-emphasized the historical Buddha and also the Four Noble Truths. What is a *bodhisattva*? A *bodhisattva* vows to attain enlightenment for the benefit of all sentient beings. It's an explicit commitment toward awakening with an added dimension, predicated on the idea of rebirth, to keep taking a human life to be of benefit to others.

To accomplish this formidable goal the *bodhisattva* must undertake six (or ten) *paramitas* (perfections): generosity, morality, patience, vigor, meditation, and wisdom. The expanded list of ten *paramitas* includes in addition to the six: skillful means, conviction, strength, and knowledge. The *bodhisattva* also pursues the five *margas* (paths) and the ten *bhumis* (grounds or stages of spiritual attainment).

Theravada

Theravada Buddhism can be traced all the way back to the First Council, shortly after Buddha's death. Theravada Buddhists claim that they have adhered to the Buddha's original teachings and are, therefore, the purest form of Buddhism. They established the Pali Canon, the teachings that were passed down orally for 400 years.

The Theravada (Doctrine of Elders) is the sole surviving school of Buddhism from the early days of Buddhism. It traces it roots back to the Buddha himself and his closest disciples. It is also known as Southern Buddhism because this is where it has flourished over the centuries: Sri Lanka, Thailand, Burma, Cambodia, and Laos. Theravada keeps its ties close to the life of the Buddha and the Pali Canon (unlike Mahayana that has introduced new texts and concepts).

Mahayana

Mahayana has been around since the Second Council, but Mahayana also can argue a direct descent from the Buddha's teachings. Mahayana Buddhists believe they split off from the Theravada tradition in order to reform the teachings and take them back to a purer form the Buddha had originally taught, although the Mahayana *sutras* such as the Perfection of Wisdom and Heart Sutra are not directly attributed to the Buddha.

Emptiness

The cardinal emphasis of Mahayana is on *shunyata*, often translated as "emptiness" or "the void." The Buddha's early teachings discuss the emptiness of self (*anatman, anatta*) and in the Mahayana this concept is expanded to everything.

Shunyata is, perhaps, the most confusing and mystical of the Buddhist concepts and the most difficult for the Western mind to grasp. Truth goes beyond dualistic distinctions and thus "emptiness is form" and "form is emptiness."

These distinctions can get you bogged down in subtle philosophical arguments. Is the world real? And what does it mean to be real? To further clarify things (or is it to complicate things?), things can be seen as conventionally real but there is an ultimate reality that underlies what is perceived.

In Mahayana tradition, when one wakes up one realizes that the *whole world* is emptiness, that emptiness is not just the self but all things, and form and emptiness are the same thing, indistinguishable from one another. It is hard to grasp this conceptually. The best way is to practice meditation and experience it for yourself.

Much as the Theravada student strives to become an *arhat*—a spiritually enlightened individual—so the Mahayana student strives to become a *bodhisattva*. Every *bodhisattva* resolves to realize the Four Great Vows:

1. Sentient beings are numberless: I vow to save them.
2. Desires are inexhaustible: I vow to put an end to them.
3. The dharmas are boundless: I vow to master them.
4. The Buddha Way is unattainable: I vow to attain it.

Three Bodies (Trikayas)

Mahayanas believe that buddhanature appears in three different forms. These bodies are the forms that the Buddha or buddhanature take. This is known as the Three Body Doctrine of compassion. As elsewhere, these bodies can be interpreted symbolically as well as literally. The three forms are:

- *Nirmanakaya* (emanation body) refers to the historical Buddha as he embodied the truth of the Dharma in a perfected form. The Buddha and the Dharma are one and the same (and you will often see this conjunction—*Buddhadharma*).
- *Sambhogakaya* (bliss body) is the idealized form of the Buddha. This "body" of the Buddha is not limited to its physical form and, in traditional thought, would occupy different realms or represent different states of consciousness. This body is experienced through intensive meditation.

- *Dharmakaya* (truth body). According to Buddhist scholar John Peacock, the "Dharmakaya is synonymous with ultimate truth and is seen as being totally transcendent and unchanging." The Dharmakaya refers to the approximation the human mind can sometimes make with reality. This body is enlightenment.

Vajrayana

Vajrayana Buddhism developed out of the Mahayana school of teachings sometime between the third and seventh centuries B.C. It is said that the Buddha practiced this esoteric tradition, but because of its advanced and special nature it didn't evolve into common practice. Vajrayana Buddhists believe the Buddha taught these practices through special texts, called *tantras*, but the tantras themselves didn't come to light until the seventh century.

Vajrayana Buddhists believe their teachings can be directly linked to the Buddha and that *they* practice the purest form of Buddhism. Vajrayana is found predominately in Tibet, a remote country, surrounded by the Himalayan Mountains, and isolated from the rest of the world. Tibetan Buddhism emerged when Mahayana Buddhism reached Tibet and it became intertwined with the native Bön folk religion.

Tantric Buddhism

Vajrayana Buddhism is also called Tantric Buddhism, "Diamond Vehicle," the "Completion Vehicle," the "Thunderbolt Vehicle," and the "Indestructible Path."

Padmasambhava, a Buddhist monk who arrived in Tibet from India, is considered one of the founders of Vajrayana Buddhism and is credited with developing many of the practices present today.

Vajrayana relies heavily on symbol and ritual, more so than other forms of Buddhism. It invokes magical deities belonging to a cosmic monastery. The practices in Vajrayana Buddhism are special and complex. The teachings are designed to bring the student to enlightenment in this lifetime; therefore the practices are intense, subtle, and difficult, and enlightenment presumably occurs more quickly than with other forms of practice. The student of the tantric practices has a teacher, called a *guru* (an enlightened teacher is a *lama*). The practices are often kept secret between the student and teacher, which adds to the mystery around the tradition.

ZEN BUDDHISM

The Core of Meditation

The origins of Zen are found in China when Bodhidharma went there in the sixth century A.D. In China it was called Chan, in Korea it was called Son, in Japan it was called Zen, all meaning "meditation." Zen offers a fresh interpretation of the Buddha's teachings and forms of practice that are straightforward and profound.

Meditation is the core practice of Zen and teachers are notorious for irreverent, unpredictable, and unorthodox methods of teaching. Zen has had a large influence on Taiwan, Korea, Vietnam, Japan, and now the West, especially America, which is now the most vital center of Zen practice in the world. Zen emphasizes enlightened masters over scriptures and is the least academic of all the Buddhist schools.

Zen is comprised of four principles:

1. Transmission outside the orthodox Buddhist teachers through its lineages
2. A belief that truth is not dependent upon established doctrine and a belief in the value of experience over the value of scripture
3. A direct point to the mind
4. An emphasis on examining one's original nature and the attainment of enlightenment

The Buddha's disciple Kashyapa (or Mahakashyapa) was the forebear of Zen. It was he alone who understood the Buddha's teaching when he held up a flower and smiled. Seeing that flower occasioned Kashyapa's enlightenment and reflects the emphasis in Zen that transmission does not require language.

Rinzai School of Zen

Rinzai emphasizes sudden enlightenment that is predicated on the fact that everyone already has *buddhanature*. The right context will bring this sudden realization of what is already there. This sudden burst of insight is called *kensho*. The Rinzai school bristles against slow and silent illumination found in *shikintaza* (just sitting). In Rinzai you meditate not to attain wisdom but as an expression of wisdom.

> *Body and mind of themselves will drop away and your original face will be manifested. If you want to attain suchness, you should practice suchness without delay.*
> —Dōgen, on *zazen* practice

Koans

Koans are designed to short circuit the rational mind and provide the basis for a sudden spiritual awakening. The most famous of these inscrutable puzzles is, "What is the sound of one hand clapping." As one Zen master said of koans, "It is the place where truth is." Koans are an important part of Rinzai practice. Students are normally assigned a koan in *dokusan* (a private meeting between the Zen master and the student).

The life of a Zen monk in Japan is arduous with rigorous periods of meditation, work practice, and exposure to the elements. It's not for the faint of heart or for those not serious about the practice or not prepared for the rigors that await them. If you show up at the gates of a Zen temple in Japan you may have to wait two days to get into the temple. This is the first test. If you pass this test, you may then sit alone in a small room for three to five days. Having passed this test you will then be admitted into the Zendo with the rest of the monks and after a few days more of practice you will then meet the Zen master.

The Eight Gates of Zen

If you study at Zen Mountain Monastery and the Zen Center of New York City (part of the Mountains and Rivers Order of Zen) you will be exposed to the Eight Gates of Zen.

1. *Zazen*: *Zazen* is the formal seated practice of meditation and the "cornerstone of Zen training."
2. Zen Study: Zen is an ancestral lineage and the Zen teacher is "indispensable in helping to navigate the difficulties along the way, directly pointing to your inherent perfection."
3. Liturgy: Is an outward manifestation of what is known intuitively and involves bowing and chanting as expressions of the truths that are cultivated in practice.
4. Art Practice: "Creativity and spirituality share a common source." Art, both traditional and contemporary, can help the practitioner, as with liturgy, to express the truths experienced in Zen practice.
5. Body Practice: Exploring the physical body as a "vehicle for self-realization." These practices range from Tai Chi to eating meals.
6. Buddhist Studies: "Academic study of Buddhist texts and commentaries is an essential part of establishing sound religious practice."
7. Work Practice: Every dimension of life can be "transformed into a sacred activity." Work practice becomes an opportunity to broaden spiritual practice.

8. Right Action: Is the study and practice of the Buddhist Precepts, "the moral and ethical teachings of the Buddha. Engaging the precepts teaches you to embody compassion as the selfless activity of the awakened mind."

Sitting

Dōgen Zenji (1200–1253) was the founder of the Soto lineage of Buddhism in Japan. Dōgen taught a way of sitting called shikantaza, which means "just sitting," nothing else—no breath counting, no koan practice at all. Shikantaza means that sitting is enlightened mind. You don't sit to become enlightened, you sit to enjoy your enlightened mind.

Group Practice

The *sangha* is key to Zen practice. The *sangha* usually meets in the *zendo*, a large hall or room where *zazen* is practiced. When a group gets together to practice, certain rules must apply to ensure that order and the quality of practice is maintained. Each practice group might have its own rules of practice and there might be some variation. Some of the practices used by a *sangha* might include: walking meditation, a dharma talk given by the teacher, tea service, *sutra* recitation, and bowing. Lighting of candles and incense might be part of the *sesshin*.

When the Student Is Ready

It is said that when the student is ready, the teacher appears. Although at the heart of Zen is the realization that you are already enlightened, the student/teacher relationship in Zen is a very important element of practice. A teacher will guide the student through the various stages of practice, helping the student toward enlightenment.

SIDDHARTHA

The Buddha Incarnate

The man who would become the Buddha can be seen as a godlike mystic, rational philosopher, psychologist, physician, or social reformer. Buddhist texts contain few references to biographical events from his life. However, historians do agree that he did actually exist and lived a long and prosperous life—he died at eighty years old after teaching for forty-five years, traveling all over India to do so. Although the Buddha's teachings were preserved through oral recitation and first written down hundreds of years after his death, they are considered credible and accurate.

Little consensus can be found among scholars on the historical facts of the Buddha's life. This is due in part to the lack of biographical detail he shared in his teachings that later became the Pali Canon. A few key moments in the Buddha's story are known. Up until recently the year of the Buddha's death was taken to be either 483 or 486 B.C. However, new evidence suggests that it might have been as late as 400 B.C. His birth would have been eighty years prior to the earlier or later date (either 566 or 563 B.C. or as late as 480 B.C.). Many of the details of the Buddha's biography come from the poem, *Buddhacharita* by Ashvogosa that was written in the second century.

Myth and Metaphor

As with the man himself, the life story of the Buddha can likewise be seen from different perspectives. Taken literally, it speaks of magic, wonder, and prophecy; viewed metaphorically it is a parable of sacrifice in the service of ultimate attainment. Certain elements of the narrative appear to provide drama to the story, but probably little in the way of historical fact. Siddhartha Gautama was born to a noble family in the Himalayan foothills, on the border of northern India and southern Nepal. Siddhartha's mother was Mahamaya, his father Suddhodhana, and he was a blessing to the childless couple as they would now have a prince and an heir to rule over the Shakya clan, their small but prosperous region of the kingdom. They named their son Siddhartha, which means "every wish fulfilled."

Noble but Not Kings

While Siddhartha Gautama is often described as a prince and his parents Queen Mahamaya and King Suddhodhana, it is more likely that his parents were part of the nobility but not monarchs. His father was a magistrate of a smaller state in the Himalayan foothills. The elevation of the family to the highest royalty may be part of the mythology that has developed around the life of the Buddha.

The Birth of the Buddha

There are many mythologies and stories surrounding the birth of the Buddha. His mother, Mahamaya, dreamt of a white elephant who entered her womb from the right side of her body. According to the legend, Mahamaya experienced a virtually pain-free delivery with the assistance of a tree that bent to offer its branches. The future Buddha exited the womb unbloodied and able to walk and talk. In some accounts, Siddhartha emerged from her right side, avoiding the "pollution" of the birth canal.

It is generally agreed upon (with some variation) that when Siddhartha was but days old, his father, Suddhodhana, invited a large group of Brahmins to a feast at the palace so that they could tell the future of the newborn baby. Eight of the Brahmins concurred on the prediction that Siddhartha would either become a great and powerful ruler of all the land, or a great spiritual teacher.

What Is a Brahmin?

The Brahmins were the priests, the highest class in the hereditary caste system of India. According to the caste system of Hinduism in ancient India, there were four classes of people: rulers and warriors (the Kshatriyas), business people and artisans (the Vaishyas), the Brahmins, and finally the unskilled laborers or untouchables (the Shudras).

They warned that if Siddhartha left the palace and saw what the real world was like he might have an existential crisis and turn toward a spiritual life. If he remained within the cloistered palace walls, he would become a great ruler of the world. One of these Brahmins, Kondanna, was convinced, however, that the young boy would become an enlightened one and warned of four signs that would influence the young Siddhartha and spur him to leave his home and commence a spiritual journey.

The Raising of the Would-Be King

According to the legend, young Siddhartha was surrounded by beautiful things and kept captive within the palace grounds so he would not be subjected to the sicknesses and poverty of the people of the kingdom. Guards were posted all around the palace grounds and Siddhartha was discouraged from leaving and protected from seeing anything distressing to his young life.

One afternoon, when Siddhartha was eight years old, he sat under the shade of a rose apple tree watching the plowing of the fields as the town prepared for the new crop. He noticed that the plowing had upset the ground and that insects had been harmed in the process. The young boy felt sadness come over him as if he were attached to the insects, as though he had experienced a personal loss. And yet the day was beautiful and the shade of the rose apple tree wonderfully cool. Joy rose up inside him and he experienced a moment of meditative bliss. The compassion and love he felt for the insects took him outside himself and he was momentarily free.

The Four Signs

Siddhartha begged his father to allow him to go beyond the palace walls. Suddhodhana hated to deny his son anything so he quickly tried to ensure that life outside the palace gates was just as perfect as life inside. When Siddhartha wandered outside, everywhere he went he saw happiness, health, and good cheer. Then suddenly an old decrepit man with white hair, withered skin, and a staff to lean on crossed his path. Leaning over to his companion and servant, Chandaka, Siddhartha asked, "What is this?"

Chandaka explained that before them was an old man and told Siddhartha that everyone would age similarly one day. Siddhartha was saddened and shocked by the sight of the old man and wondered how he could continue to enjoy such sights as his garden when such suffering was to come later.

What's It Mean?

Buddha is also sometimes referred to as *Shakyamuni*, which means "Sage of the Shakya Clan," as he hailed from Shakya.

He decided to "go forth" into the world the night he was born. Legend has it that he snuck out of the palace when everyone fell asleep, including, mysteriously, the palace guards. He vowed to live an unfettered existence. Family was not part of the life of a spiritual seeker, he had to go forth alone. The thought of losing his family forever to old age and death must have been a very powerful catalyst for such dramatic change. He was motivated to go forth to find an end to suffering, by whatever means necessary, for the benefit of his family and for all of humanity.

Finding the Way

Siddhartha became a seeker of truth, called a *shramana*. These ascetics were not seen as beggars and dropouts; to seek a holy life was a worthy cause. The young prince set out to find himself a teacher, and wandered far and wide over the Ganges plain, learning what he could from the available *gurus* (teachers).

Siddhartha was a meditation prodigy and quickly reached very high states of meditation (called *dhyanas* or *jhanas* in Pali). However, once he left the profound state of meditative absorption he found himself back in the realm of suffering. In an attempt to go beyond it, he adopted a severe asceticism, taking only a grain of rice or drinking mud for sustenance each day. He wore little or no clothing, slept out in the open no matter the weather, starved himself beyond measure, and even ingested his own waste matter. He lay on the most uncomfortable surfaces possible and inflicted severe deprivation on himself, convinced that external suffering would banish the internal suffering forever. But still he was plagued with desires and cravings. After seven long years of effort he was close to death.

Moderate effort over a long time is important, no matter what you are trying to do. One brings failure on oneself by working extremely hard at the beginning, attempting to do too much, and then giving it all up after a short time.
—The Dalai Lama

Fortunately, a young girl named Sujata offered him some rice porridge and he took it, breaking his vows of asceticism. This was the beginning of his awakening and finding the middle path between the extremes of sensual indulgence and dangerous denial of his physical needs. He recalled his meditation experience under the rose apple tree and realized there was another way to accomplish his goal. With the strength gained from that meal, the emaciated Siddhartha sat beneath a pipal tree and made a new vow: to not get up until he had found what he was looking for.

The Tree of Awakening

The pipal tree—the tree under which Buddha sat—comes from the Asiatic fig tree, and became known as the Bodhi Tree, the tree of "awakening." Today, a descendant of the original Bodhi Tree sits just where Buddha sat approximately 2,500 years ago. Followers of Buddhism visit the tree and meditate, hoping to achieve an enlightened mind just like Buddha.

Awakening

As he nursed himself back to health, Siddhartha became very conscious of his movements in the world and paid close attention to how he reacted to his environment, watching his thoughts as they passed through his mind. He became aware of the movements he made while he ate, slept, and walked. Siddhartha slowly became mindful of his every gesture and thought. Mindfulness is the process of bringing attention to the present moment, away from thoughts of the future or the past or judgments about the present. It's making contact with the lived experience of now. Mindfulness made Siddhartha aware of every craving that passed through him and of how transitory these cravings were. Everything changed: Everything came and everything passed.

He began to notice that all things were interrelated. The fruit was attached to the tree that was attached to the earth that received nutrients from the sky when it rained. The earth nourished the insects and animals, which ate the berries that came from the trees that came from the earth that were nourished by the sky. The animals died, the plants died, and so would Siddhartha. Life was filled with interconnectedness and change. And impermanence. Everything that existed would die. He would die, his thoughts would die, his desires would die. The moment would die, and another would be born in its place.

Whether or not he worried about loss, loss was inevitable as change was inevitable. With change came fear. And with fear came *dukkha*.

A Man of Many Names

Siddhartha is known by many names, including: Siddhartha Gautama (in Pali his name his Siddhattha Gotoma), his birth and family name; Shakyamuni, Sage of the Shakya Clan; Buddha, the Fully Awakened One; and Tathagata, the Thus-Perfected One or the One Who Has Found the Truth.

Enlightenment

As he sat under the Bodhi Tree, meditating and watching his thoughts come and go, his mind started to break free of the constraints of his ego. He entered each moment fully present as his thoughts dropped away.

During his time under the tree, the Buddha was tempted by his enemy Mara, who can be seen as a metaphor for desire. Undeterred, Siddhartha persisted with his meditation, transforming Mara's forces into flowers that rained petals down upon his head.

The legend says that after his time under the pipal tree, Siddhartha had changed. When he encountered other people they could sense this change. Soon after the Buddha attained enlightenment, he walked by a man, a fellow traveler. The man was struck by the Buddha's unusual radiance and peaceful demeanor.

"My friend, what are you?" he asked the Buddha. "Are you a god?"

"No," answered the Buddha.

"Are you some kind of magician?"

"No," the Buddha answered again.

"Are you a man?"

"No."

"Well, my friend, then what are you?"

The Buddha replied, "I am buddho (awake).

And so the name stuck and Siddhartha became the *Buddha*.

CHAPTER 8
OTHER FAITHS

Beyond the five major world religious traditions lies a vast sea of belief and practice. Some religious groups have begun as obscure sects and risen to worldwide faiths with millions of committed followers. Others have remained small and isolated, never gathering more than several hundred or thousand adherents, yet deeply convinced of their spiritual message.

The religious impulse has been part of the human psyche from its earliest evolution. From the cave drawings in Lascaux, France, to the Great Pyramid of Giza, from Haitian Vodou to Sikhism, Jainism, and Swedenborgianism, religion shows human creativity and spirituality in all its many facets.

MORMONISM

The Message of Moroni

The Church of Jesus Christ of Latter Day Saints is the principal formal body embracing Mormonism. It has a membership of nearly 15 million members and is headquartered in Salt Lake City, Utah. The next largest Mormon denomination is the Reorganized Church of Jesus Christ of Latter Day Saints, which is headquartered in Independence, Missouri. It has a membership of more than a quarter of a million.

Joseph Smith (1805–1844) founded Mormonism in upstate New York after he translated his revelation of *The Book of Mormon*, which recounts the history of certain tribes of Israel that migrated to America before Christ was born. They apparently underwent experiences similar to those written in the Old Testament. Mormons accept the Bible only "as far as it is translated correctly," because Joseph Smith did not finish his translation. However, he did produce another scripture called *The Pearl of Great Price*.

A major difference between the two sects is that the Reorganized Church, while holding to *The Book of Mormon*, rejects certain parts of it, in particular the evolutionary concepts of deity and polytheism, the new covenant of celestial marriage, baptism on behalf of the dead, polygamy, and tithing. They also reject *The Book of Abraham* because they do not believe it is of divine origin.

The Mormons were established by Joseph Smith on April 6, 1830, after revelations he received from the angel Moroni. The church grew rapidly but incurred the suspicion and dislike of many, including the U.S. government, which objected to the church's advocacy and practice of polygamy.

The church was driven from state to state as Smith attempted to found a permanent Mormon settlement. Finally, on June 27, 1844, Smith and his brother were murdered by a mob in Carthage, Illinois. Under the new leadership of Brigham Young (1801–1877), the Mormons moved west, and in 1847 he and others established themselves on the shores of the Great Salt Lake in the Utah territory. Conflict with the government continued, but eventually Young agreed to step down in favor of a U.S.-appointed governor of the territory. After vigorous prosecution by the government, in 1890 the church abolished the institution of polygamy and thereafter grew in power and influence in Utah and surrounding states.

Way of Life

The Mormon way of life is distinguished by order and respect for authority, church activism, strong conformity with the group, and vigorous proselytizing and missionary activities. As an example of the strictness of the faith, the official pamphlet on *Dating and Courtship* calls passionate kissing prior to marriage a sin. The church advises young people not to engage in any behavior with anyone that they would not do with a brother or sister while in the presence of their parents. The church also discourages interracial dating, although its position on this has begun to change over the past decade.

As for military service, the church considers it a duty of its members. However, any member can opt for conscientious objection, but not by giving the church as a reason for it. The church discourages conscientious objection, and in fact, endorses a corps of chaplains who serve in the United States armed services.

Mormons believe that faithful members of the church will inherit eternal life as gods, and even those who had rejected God's law would live in glory.

Secret Polygamy

There have been Mormon splinter groups that adopted polygamist marriage practices in spite of the church's renunciation of them in 1890. Some of those groups in Utah and northern Arizona continued the practice in secret.

Divisions and Teachings

Basically, the Mormons are divided into what are called stakes, which usually have about 5,000 members and are run by a stake president. Within each stake are wards comprised of a few hundred members, under a lay clergyman. It is through this structured administration that the church regulates the lives of its members. At the high end, presiding over the entire church, is a supreme council of three high priests, called the First Presidency or the president and his counselors. Next are twelve apostles, who are equal in authority to the First Presidency. Essentially, those officers run the show.

In addition to the semiannual general conferences, stake and ward conferences are held; included in these are, of course, the usual Sabbath meetings. It is at these meetings that the consent of the people has to be obtained before any important actions are taken.

The Mormon Church is supported by tithes and offerings from its members. The money is used to support the church and its missionaries in the field.

There is an accent on teaching the philosophy of the faith in Sabbath schools and young ladies' mutual improvement associations, which are primarily religious in nature and offer support for the unfortunate. A group called the Relief Society is a women's organization that has a special mission for the relief of the destitute and the care of the sick.

The Church of Latter Day Saints is world famous for its genealogy repository, the Family History Library in Salt Lake City. It boasts more than 2 billion names and is considered the finest such repository in the world. The church has made available, free to church members and nonmembers alike, over 600 million names for research purposes on its FamilySearch website on the Internet. It encourages its members to trace their ancestors as a religious obligation. This service is now available to anyone.

PENTECOSTALISM

An American Christianity

Probably the most common words that come to mind when one thinks of Pentecostalism is the phrase "speaking in tongues," as well as the names Aimee Semple McPherson and, more recently, Oral Roberts.

The origins of Pentecostalism go back to the Bible and the Jewish pilgrimage festival of Pentecost. Early Christians believed that Pentecost commemorated the day the Holy Spirit descended in fulfillment of the promise of Jesus. In Acts 2:2–13 it is written:

> *And suddenly a sound came from heaven like the rush of a mighty wind, and it filled all the house where they were sitting. And there appeared to them tongues as of fire distributed and resting on each one of them. And they were filled with the Holy Spirit and began to speak in other tongues, as the Spirit gave them utterance. Now there were dwelling in Jerusalem Jews, devoted men from every nation under heaven. And at this sound the multitude came together, and they were bewildered, because each one heard them speaking in his own language. And they were amazed and wondered, saying, "Are not all these who are speaking Galileans: And how is it that we hear, each of us in his own language?"*
>
> *And all were amazed and perplexed, saying to one another, "What does this mean?" But others mocking, said, "They are filled with new wine."*

Pentecostalism arose out of Protestantism in the twentieth century due to dissension with the rigid manner in which the established churches preached and organized the delivery of their way of interpreting the Bible.

Pentecostalists endorse a more literal interpretation of the Bible than mainstream Christians. Many churches have adopted specific passages as their guiding force. One such passage is found in Mark 16:15–20 where it is reported that those who receive baptism and find salvation will "cast out devils, speak in strange tongues; if they handle snakes or drink deadly poison they will come to no harm; and the sick on whom they lay their hands will recover." There are some churches that include the handling of deadly snakes and the drinking of poison as part of their worship services.

The new sect didn't think the way of the true Christians was memorizing prayers and creeds and adhering to hard and fast rules within an unwavering structure. The Pentecostalists sought a direct experience of God that would produce a sense of ecstasy, known as the baptism of the Holy Spirit. This baptism was seen as a second blessing.

Speaking in Tongues

It was in Topeka, Kansas, in 1901 at a service being conducted at the Kansas Bible College by Charles Fox Parham (1873–1929) that the movement—it is more than a denomination—got the first demonstration of a strange happening. A female participant was praying and suddenly began speaking what seemed to be a foreign language. Apparently she was unable to speak English for three days afterward. This event had a dramatic effect not only on Parham but also the entire congregation. The demonstration was taken as a sign from God and the word quickly spread.

Coincidentally, at the same time in Los Angeles a black preacher, William Joseph Seymour (1870–1922), started preaching at a mission and it wasn't long until he and his parishioners were speaking in unknown tongues. A church was founded on Azusa Street in Los Angeles, and it grew rapidly as services began to be held on a regular basis.

Women in Pentecostalism

Women became active members in the Pentecostal movement. One of them, Aimee Semple McPherson (1890–1944), generated a big following from her tabernacle where she produced theatrically dramatic versions of biblical stories from the stage.

The speaking in tongues, known as glossolalia, was not universally accepted; in fact, it was quite the reverse for a lot of people. As in the biblical story in Acts, many people thought the speakers were drunk. It wasn't just the fact of speaking in an unintelligible tongue that upset listeners, it was the emotional overtones that went with the delivery. The term *holy rollers* was ascribed to practitioners who were actually rolling in the aisles of the church in their ecstasy. Adherents believed that speaking in tongues and the actions that went with it were a way of communicating directly with God. However, no reliable sources have established that an actual language was or is being uttered during glossolalia.

Expansion
Pentecostalism is now one of the fastest-growing religious movements in the world. In the United States alone it claims 9

million adherents; worldwide, the figure goes up to 400 million. It is sometimes referred to as "the third force of Christianity."

The movement first drew members from among the poor, not the establishment; the promise of equality for all was particularly attractive to the unfortunate. Thus, the movement became associated with the Bible Belt in the Southern states among poor whites and urban blacks. It then became increasingly popular with the middle classes around the country, and once the movement spread to the mainstream of society, members of churches such as the Episcopal, Lutheran, and Presbyterian adopted it, often in addition to their own religion.

The Power of the Lord

In 1913, at a Pentecostal meeting in California, John G. Scheppe announced that he had experienced the power of Jesus. Enough people accepted his statement for them to proclaim that true baptism can come only in the name of Jesus and not the trinity. The justification for this, they said, could be found in the Bible, John 3:5 and Acts 2:38.

The controversy split the movement and led to the formation of new sects within Pentecostalism. Three main movements evolved: Pentecostalism, Fundamentalism, and Evangelicalism. Other sects, particularly throughout the rest of the world, are emerging.

Beliefs, Worship, Writings, and Rites

Pentecostals have not united into a single denomination in spite of believing in baptism of the spirit and common beliefs in selected doctrines of the Christian faiths. They have strong beliefs in the literal interpretation of the Bible and healing by the spirit.

The history of Pentecostalism shows that many adherents either added it to their original faith or left the original faith entirely. There is gathering literature from Roman Catholics who have become committed to Pentecostalism.

Catholics tend to investigate Pentecostalism with a view of trying to distinguish what is different about it today from its historical standpoint. With the growth of Pentecostalism, the charismatic experience, as it is called, has expanded its presence into many parts of the world to such an extent that it is being looked at by some as a new era of the spirit. The Pentecostalists envision the movement sweeping whole countries, cultures, and religions, including Catholicism, with a promise of changing Christianity. They have even coined a new name: Catholic Pentecostals. The Pentecostalist viewpoint is that there is confusion not only in Catholicism but also in Christianity. This opinion is not shared by the Roman Catholic Church and other Christian denominations.

Shaking for God

On Father's Day in 1995 at the Brownsville Assembly of God in Pensacola, Florida, a revival was held. During a prayer service congregants began falling about and shaking. It was reported that one minister touched another on the forehead and that man fell to the ground struck dumb as if by the Holy Spirit. Thousands began to arrive, either to indulge or to watch.

Opponents of the movement say that Pentecostal-style religion is not easily captured in a denominational form because it stresses the impulse of the moment and behavior such as speaking in tongues. Many point out that similar evangelical outpourings that took place in the 1980s ended with the disgrace of people like Jimmy Swaggart and Jim and Tammy Faye Bakker.

Pentecostalists describe themselves as believing in exorcism, speaking in tongues, faith healing, and seeking supernatural experiences.

As with other developing religions, many schisms have occurred that resulted in the setting up of separate sects with their own variations of the basic belief. Here are some of the best-known Pentecostal sects:

- Church of God in Christ
- International Church of the Foursquare Gospel
- Church of God of Prophecy
- Pentecostal Holiness Church
- Fire-Baptized Holiness Church
- Pentecostal Free Will Baptist Church
- The Assemblies of God
- The United Pentecostal Church

WICCA

In 1692, an infamous trial was held in Salem, Massachusetts. Nine-year-old Elizabeth Parris, the daughter, and eleven-year-old Abigail Williams, the niece, of a Salem Village minister began to exhibit strange behavior, such as blasphemous screaming, convulsive seizures, and so on. Several other Salem girls began to demonstrate similar behavior. Physicians concluded that the girls were under the influence of Satan.

Pressured to identify some source of their afflictions, the girls named three women, and warrants were issued for their arrests. The women were examined and found guilty of witchcraft. This set in motion hysteria among the populace, which resulted in the death of twenty-four people accused of being witches; twenty were executed, the others died in prison. There is today the Salem Witch Museum and other local sites and documents that can be visited and studied.

Witchcraft and sorcery are frequently misunderstood; the two are separate entities. A witch, who is a female (a male witch is called a warlock), is someone who has innate magical powers. A sorcerer is someone who uses potions and spells to get his or her way.

No Witch by Choice

Witches are not always aware that they are witches, nor do they choose this role for themselves. So, you never know, you might pass someone on the street one day who touches you very lightly on your sleeve as you go by, and unbeknownst to both of you a spell has been passed on.

Throughout history the calamities that people are subject to are often blamed on someone else, when all the time it's his or her own doing. This common fault in human nature was, and is today, the basic motivation of prejudice: Find a scapegoat and blame someone else for what's wrong. The Christian witch-hunts of the sixteenth and seventeenth centuries were a time when thousands of witches were persecuted and executed, usually by burning them to death. While it's difficult to believe, between 1994 and 1995 more than 200 people in South Africa were burnt to death after being accused of witchcraft. Even today the Harry Potter books, which have given wonderful pleasure to thousands of children and adults, have been condemned by certain Christian fundamentalists.

Central Beliefs

Wicca is the witches' religion, said to derive from an ancient Celtic society that is older than Christianity. Other sources say the religion is a modern one that does not have a long historical connection. Either way, Wiccans were, and are, seen by the churches as having ties to Satan, which they did, and do strongly deny. They insist that Wiccans are no more like Satanists than Buddhists, Hindus, or Muslims. Modern Wiccans maintain that present-day Wicca was created by the merging of some of the ancient Celtic beliefs, deity structure, and seasonal days of celebration, with modern material from ceremonial magic.

The general belief is that Wicca arose as an important movement in England during the 1950s. The movement has claimed a fast-track expansion into North America and Europe. Some estimates put the number of adherents at 800,000 in the United States alone. That's at best an estimate because Wiccans are, understandably, reticent about telling people of their beliefs. Imagine someone at a company meeting standing up and saying he had to go because he was late for a meeting at his coven, essentially announcing he was a warlock. Not quite the same as being late for a meeting of the Sunday school choir.

If the adherent figures are true, that would make Wicca one of the largest and fastest-growing minority religions in the United States. However, it is doubtful if the correct figures will be ever be known or substantiated. Wiccans see themselves as victimized, more so than any other religious group.

Covens

Wiccans worship in a coven. Traditionally, a coven consists of thirteen people. It is preferred that the makeup of the group is six couples who are emotionally connected. The thirteenth member will be the High Priestess or Priest. Generally, there are no rules about the group, it can be mixed gender or not. However, some covens do have one gender, for instance Dianic Witches. Typically, covens meet in private homes or meeting rooms. On some occasions, holidays in particular, they meet out of doors. Nights of the full or new moon are times of choice.

Legal Recognition

A recent development has been made that allows witches and covens to become legally recognized. Churches, seminaries, and antidefamation leagues have been formed.

Covens don't advertise for members; they come through word-of-mouth recommendation and have to be unanimously approved by all the members of the coven before they become full members themselves. It might be asked that if witchcraft is so secret, how does one find a coven? Basically, the advice is networking, something the Internet has made much easier. New Age stores also often provide a meeting place for those interested in Wicca.

As an alternative to trying to find a coven, a person might prefer to learn about becoming a solitary witch or warlock. Many prospective adherents do this. Once a person feels well informed and confident enough, he or she could perform a spell to act as a kind of personal beacon to draw others of like mind. Traditional Celtic jewelry could also be worn—for instance, crescent moon earrings or a Celtic pentagram.

Religion 101 Question

What's the ideal number of members in a Wiccan coven?

Thirteen.

Practices

Witchcraft members adhere strictly to an ethical code called "Wiccan Rede." They believe that whatever they do comes back to them threefold. Thus, if they did harm they would get harm back to the power of three. Therefore, they have no incentive to curse anyone; the curse would come back to haunt them three times over. All witches practice some form of ritual magic, which must be considered "good magic." Their ethical code is spelled out in the saying: "An' it harm none, do what thou wilt."

Calling oneself "Witch" does not make a witch, but neither does heredity itself, or the collecting of titles, degrees and initiations. A witch seeks to control forces within her/himself that make life

possible in order to live wisely and well,
without harm to others, and in harmony with nature.
—The Council of American Witches, *Principles of Belief*

A deep respect for the environment features strongly in Wiccan religious activity. So, too, does the value of the feminine and the need to balance what many women, witches or not, consider the overly oppressive practice of masculine domination in traditional religions.

Witches generally worship a god and goddess, seen as different aspects of the same deity. The deity is known as the ultimate omnipotent god force in the universe and is the same God most people worship. However, witches relate better to both a mother and father figure, which is why the name *goddess* figures predominately in the craft.

Religion 101 Question

How do witches cast spells?

Typically, a witch will start a spell by casting a circle, burning some incense, lighting a special candle, then doing some rhythmic chanting.

Rituals

Wiccans have many rituals; one of the most charming is called handfasting. The ceremony was derived from the medieval wedding practices used in Scotland, Wales, and Ireland. Handfasting is basically a marriage ceremony, although it may not be a permanent state unless a valid marriage license has been obtained and a licensed priest is present at the ceremony and legally certified.

Originally, the ceremony was not considered a wedding, but a declaration of intent to marry. If, after a year and a day, the couple are still committed to each other, then they would be legally married at an official ceremony.

Before the ceremony can begin, the area chosen is traditionally swept free of debris and negativity by the Maiden of the Broom; once that's done the ceremony commences. The actual ceremony follows in a fairly traditional manner, although like Christian marriages, for instance, the couple may personalize it. The Wiccan ceremony starts with the High Priestess circling three times and incanting:

> *Three times round,*
> *Once for the Daughter,*
> *Twice for the Crone,*
> *Thrice for the Mother,*
> *who sits on the throne.*

Everything proceeds with the giving of the vows, the placing of wedding bands, and giving thanks to the elements. The ceremony ends with the opening stanza being repeated.

Festivals

Based on the Celtic calendar, the Wiccan calendar recognizes two seasons, winter and summer, each of which begins with a celebration. The eight major holidays are called the Eight Sabbats. Some covens may follow the festivals, others may have alternatives. Minor holidays are called the Lesser Sabbats.

Note that the dates given in the list below may vary:

- Yule. The Winter Solstice, December 21. The Sun God is born at Yule.
- Imbolg (also called Imbolc), February 1/2. The first signs of waking up from winter (also known as Groundhog Day).
- Ostara. The Vernal Equinox, March 22. The magical times when day and night are equal.
- Beltane, May 1. A great fertility celebration (also known as May Day).
- Litha. The Summer Solstice, June 21. It is also known as Midsummer and St. John's Day.
- Lughnasadh, August 1. The beginning of the harvest season.
- Mabon. The Autumn Equinox, September 22. A time to give thanks for the earth's bounty.
- Samhain, November 1. Samhain is the New Year's Day of the Wiccan calendar. Just as the Wiccan day of celebration begins at sundown, so the year begins with the beginning of the dark half of the year.

RASTAFARIANISM

The Lion of Judah

The origins of Rastafarianism go back to Marcus Garvey (1887–1940), one of the early founders of the Pan-Africanist movement. Garvey preached that his followers would return to Africa; he predicted that a future black African king would lead the people.

In 1930, Ras Tafari Makonnen (1892–1975) was crowned king of Ethiopia. He claimed the title Emperor Haile Selassie I (Lion of the Tribe of Judah, Elect of God, and King of Kings of Ethiopia). Thus, Haile Selassie fulfilled the prediction of a black king. As far as the Rastafarians were concerned, he was the living God for the black race. They believed that he was the Jesus Christ that Christianity speaks of, that the white man tricked the world into believing that Jesus was a white man.

Jamaica

Jamaica was sighted by Christopher Columbus in 1494; years later it was colonized by the Spanish, and subsequently by the British. The slave trade, which was introduced by the Spanish, continued on until the 1830s when it was abolished. In 1959, Jamaica became an independent country within the British Commonwealth.

It was after Haile Selassie was crowned that Rastafarianism came into being. One of its early leaders was Leonard Howell (1898–1981), who was later arrested by the Jamaican government for preaching a revolutionary doctrine. Here are his six principles:

1. Hatred for the white race.
2. The complete superiority of the black race.
3. Revenge on whites for their wickedness.
4. The negation, persecution, and humiliation of the government and legal bodies of Jamaica.
5. The preparation to go back to Africa.
6. Acknowledging Emperor Haile Selassie as the Supreme Being and only ruler of black people.

On April 21, 1966, Haile Selassie visited Jamaica. Two things resulted from his visit: April 21 was declared a special holy day, and Selassie strongly advised Rastafarians not to immigrate to Ethiopia, urging them to liberate the people of Jamaica first. Many people have since wondered about his motive for discouraging immigration. It's possible that he saw the possible immigration of thousands of Jamaicans to Ethiopia as causing far more problems than it would solve.

Rastafarians (sometimes called Rastas) do not accept that Haile Selassie is dead. They believe that his atoms have spread throughout the world and live through individual Rastafarians. The Rastafarian name for God is Jah.

Central Beliefs and Holy Writings

The original belief system of Rastafarianism was so vague that what was part of its doctrine was largely a matter of individual interpretation. Rastafarians accept the Bible, but with reservations. They think that much of the translation into English has produced distortions so that while the basic text may be in order, it should be viewed in a critical light. They have no holy scriptures, apart from the Rastafarian interpretation of the Bible.

The doctrine of Rastafarians has similarities to Christianity in that they believe that God revealed himself in Moses, their first savior, followed by Elijah and then Jesus Christ. But sources differ. One of them asserted that Rastafarians believed that Haile Selassie was actually Jesus Christ. Others believe that the devil is actually the god of the white man.

What's It Mean?

The expression "I and I" is frequently heard in the Rasta dialect. It means that all are absolutely equal. This means that people wouldn't say "you and I," but "I and I."

The two major symbols that exemplify the Rastafarians, as well as identify them, are dreadlocks and *ganja* (marijuana). Dreadlocks symbolize the Rasta roots. They are the antithesis of the blond look of the white man and his establishment. The way the hair grows and is tended represents the Lion of Judah (Haile Selassie). By association this has come to represent priesthood. As is probably well-known, dreadlocks have been adopted by many black people (and even some white people) even though they may not be adherents of Rastafarianism.

Ganja is the Rasta name for marijuana; it is used for religious purposes, and its religious justification is based on different verses from the Bible:

- "He causeth the grass for the cattle, and herb for the service of man." (Psalms 104:14)
- "Thou shalt eat the herb of the field." (Genesis 3:18)
- "Eat every herb of the land." (Exodus 10:12)
- "Better is a dinner of herb where love is, than a stalled ox and hatred therewith." (Proverbs 15:17)

The use of the herb among Rastafarians is extensive, and not only for religious ceremony. The Nyabingi celebration, for instance, uses the herb for medicinal purposes, such as for colds.

The use of *ganja* for religious rituals started in a cult commune set up by Leonard Howell in the hills of St. Catherine called Pinnacle, which overlooked the city of Kingston.

The growth of Rastafarianism is attributed to the worldwide acceptance of a reggae artist, Bob Marley (1945–1981), who became a prophet of the belief in 1975. The movement spread, mainly to black youth throughout the Caribbean, many of whom saw it as a symbol of their rebelliousness. The expansion also found believers in England and the United States.

SCIENTOLOGY

The Hollywood Celebrity Religion

Scientology developed in the 1950s as an extension of a best-selling book, *Dianetics: The Modern Science of Mental Health* by science fiction author L. Ron Hubbard (1911–1986). The book detailed Hubbard's new form of psychotherapy and became widely popular. In 1952, after developing extensive disagreements with others in the dianetics organization, Hubbard founded the Hubbard Association of Scientologists International.

Hubbard has excited considerable controversy. He was a prolific writer of science fiction and, according to his own account, spent time as a highly decorated officer in the navy, an explorer of the Far East, and for a time an adherent of an occult group in California. According to others who have investigated his biography, he performed poorly in the navy and was never decorated, probably made up the stories about exploring China and Tibet, and spent much of his time writing and making up fictions about himself.

No God?

The words *god*, *sacred deity*, *holy deity*, or any similar descriptive name does not appear in any text that is part of Scientology literature.

The Church of Scientology was formally established in the United States in 1954. It was subsequently incorporated in Great Britain and other countries. It is considered a religio-scientific movement.

The movement has generated considerable controversy, even extreme anger, with accusations of being dangerous and vicious, fleecing its members, and harassing those who disagree with its philosophy and manner of operation.

At *www.scientology.org*, a section titled "What Is Scientology?" says in part:

> *Comparing specific Scientology doctrines and practices with those of other religions, similarities and differences emerge which make it clear that although Scientology is entirely new, its origins are as ancient as religious thought itself.*
>
> *. . . And because the principles of Scientology encompass the entire scope of life, the answers it provides apply to all existence and have broad ranging applicability.*

Controversies Concerning Scientology

The Church of Scientology and its officers have had many private lawsuits brought against them. The government prosecuted the movement for fraud, tax evasion, financial mismanagement, and conspiracy to steal government documents. The church claimed that it was being persecuted by government agencies and in retaliation has filed thousands of its own lawsuits against the government and private individuals. Former members testified that Hubbard was guilty of using a tax-exempt church status to build a thriving, profitable business.

Central Beliefs

The core of the movement is based on a system of psychology and the way the mind seems to work. The word *engram* is part of the Scientology nomenclature; it means a memory trace that is supposedly a permanent change in the brain that accounts for the existence of a memory that is not available to the conscious mind. However, it remains dormant in the subconscious, and can be brought into consciousness when triggered by new experiences. These new experiences are supplied in what Scientology calls an audit, which is conducted by an auditor in a one-on-one session with a potential devotee where the auditor confronts the engram in order to bring it to the surface and clear, or free, the devotee's mind of it. The purpose is to free the mind of engrams and thus allow the devotee to achieve improved mental health and outlook. Those familiar with the techniques originated by Sigmund Freud might find similarities.

To quote again from official statements: "An auditor is a minister or minister-in-training of the Church of Scientology. *Auditor* means one who listens, from the Latin *audire* meaning "to hear or listen." An auditor is a person trained and qualified in applying auditing to individuals for their betterment. An auditor works together with the preclear (a person who has not yet completed the clearing process) to help him or her defeat his or her reactive mind."

The officially stated Scientology meaning of the word *engram* is, "A recording made by the reactive mind when a person is unconscious." An engram is not a memory, it is a particular type of mental image that is a complete recording, down to the last accurate details, of every perception present in a moment of partial or full unconsciousness. "To become 'clear' indicates a highly desirable state for the individual, achieved through auditing, which was never attainable before Dianetics. A Clear is a person who no longer has his own reactive mind and therefore suffers none of the ill effects that the reactive mind can cause. The Clear has no engrams, which when restimulated, throw out the correctness of his computations by entering hidden and false data."

In addition to the personal mental freeing that supposedly takes place, Scientology lays great stress on a universal life energy, what they call thetan.

One unusual feature of Scientology, as compared with other religions, is that those progressing through the different levels, seeking to attain Clear status, have to pay for the process—something that can run to hundreds of thousands of dollars. Part of the controversy regarding the church is precisely the fact that in no other religion do adherents have to pay for the privilege of receiving the faith's benefits.

The Works of L. Ron Hubbard

L. Ron Hubbard has described his philosophy in more than 5,000 writings and in 3,000 tape-recorded lectures. *Dianetics: The Modern Science of Mental Health* has been described by the movement as marking a turning point in history. There are no sacred texts.

Worship and Practices

The movement appoints its own ministers. Scientology ministers perform the same types of ceremonies and services that ministers and priests of other religions perform. At a weekly service a sermon may be given that addresses the idea that a person is a spiritual being.

Scientologist Celebrities

Scientology has been vigorous in its attempts to recruit celebrities, especially from the entertainment world. Among the prominent Scientologist celebrities are:

- Tom Cruise
- John Travolta
- Kirstie Alley
- Anne Archer
- Nancy Cartwright
- Jenna Elfman
- Juliette Lewis
- Bijou Phillips
- Giovanni Ribisi
- Greta Van Susteren

Scientology congregations celebrate weddings and christenings with their own formal ceremonies and mark the passing of their fellows with funeral rites.

The chaplain also ministers to Scientologists on a personal level. Apparently such aid can take many forms. It is stated that Scientology is a religion where, ultimately, everyone wins. An escalating fee structure for services rendered is stringently applied.

APPENDIX

TIMELINE OF
IMPORTANT DATES

What follows is an overview calendar of some of the important dates in the history of religion. It is not meant to be exhaustive, but it should provide a general reference to the emergence of important people and events. It should also provide a good indication of the dissension between religions that took place over the centuries. Please note that the dates given in the B.C. time period are, even among scholars, frequently educated guesstimates.

2000–1501—Stonehenge, England is the center of religious worship.

1500–1001—Moses is given the Ten Commandments on Mount Sinai.

1100–500—The Veda, sacred texts of the Hindus, are compiled.

800–701--Isaiah teaches of the coming of the Messiah.

600–501—Confucius, Buddha, Zoroaster, Lao-tse, and the Jewish prophets are at their height.

540–468—Mahavira establishes Jainism. Siddhartha Gautama, the founder of Buddhism, is born.

450–401—The Torah becomes the moral essence of the Jews.

200—The Bhagavad Gita is written.

The year 1—Believed to be the birth of Jesus of Nazareth, founder of Christianity.

A.D.

30—Probable date of the crucifixion and death of Jesus Christ.

51–100—St. Peter, disciple of Jesus, is executed. First four books of the New Testament, the gospels according to Matthew, Mark, Luke, and John, believed written.

570—Muhammad, the founder of Islam, is born.

622—Muhammad flees persecution in Mecca and settles in Yathrib (later Madinah). Marks year one in the Muslim calendar.

625—Muhammad begins to dictate the Qur'an.

632—Buddhism becomes the state religion of Tibet.

695—Persecution of the Jews in Spain.

936—Traditional date of the arrival in India from Iran of the first Parsis (followers of Zoroastrianism).

1054—The split between the Roman Catholic Church and Eastern Orthodox Church becomes permanent.

1200—Islam begins to replace Indian religions.

1229—The Inquisition in Toulouse, France, bans the reading of the Bible by all laymen.

1252—The Inquisition begins to use instruments of torture.

1306—The Jews are expelled from France.

1309—The Roman Catholic papacy is seated in Avignon, France.

1349—Persecution of the Jews in Germany.

1483—Martin Luther, who becomes leader of the Protestant Reformation in Germany, is born.

1491—Ignatius Loyola, founder of the Jesuit Order of Roman Catholic priests, is born.

1492—The Jews are given three months by the Inquisitor General of Spain to accept Christianity or leave the country.

1507—Martin Luther is ordained.

1509—John Calvin, leader of the Protestant Reformation in France, is born.

1509—Emperor Maximilian I orders the confiscation and destruction of all Jewish books, including the Torah.

1531—The Inquisition in Portugal.

1549—Only the new Book of Prayer allowed to be used in England.

1561—French Calvinist refugees from Flanders settle in England.

1611—The authorized version of the King James Bible is published.

1620—The Pilgrim fathers leave Plymouth, England, in the *Mayflower* for North America. They settle at New Plymouth, Mass., and establish the Plymouth Colony.

1642—George Fox, English founder of the Protestant Society of Friends (the Quakers), is born.

1703—John Wesley, English founder of the Protestant movement that later became the Methodist Church, is born.

1716—Christian religious teaching banned in China.

1859—Charles Darwin, English naturalist, publishes *Origin of Species*.

1869—Meeting of the first Roman Catholic Vatican Council, at which the dogma of papal infallibility is advocated.

1869—Mohandas K. Gandhi, who helped his country achieve independence from Britain and sought rapprochement between Hindus and Muslims, is born.

1933—The persecution and extermination of European Jews, known as the Holocaust, by Adolf Hitler's Nazi party begins.

1948—The independent Jewish state of Israel comes into existence.

1952—The Revised Standard Version of the Bible reaches number one on the nonfiction bestseller lists.

1962—Meeting of the second Roman Catholic Vatican Council, at which changes were made in the liturgy and greater participation in services by lay church members was encouraged.

1983—The World Council of Churches establishes new levels of consensus in regard to Christian faith and worship. The Council holds a historic interdenominational Eucharist.

1990—The New Revised Standard Version of the Bible is published.

INDEX